Student's Book Answer Key

1.1 2 is 3 are 4 is 5 are 6 am

1.2 2 My grandparents aren't very old. 3 It isn't fun to hang out with my brothers. 4 My mum isn't a brilliant cook! 5 Terry's grandmother isn't ninety-nine! 6 They aren't sorry about the argument.

1.3 2 Am I your best friend? Yes, you are. 3 Is Annabel your mum? No, she isn't. 4 Are Kenny and Kyle twins? No, they aren't. 5 Is Jess's stepfather nice? Yes, he is. 6 Is it important to be kind to your friends? Yes, it is.

1.4 Possible answers: 3 Fred and Wilma are husband and wife. 4 Leo and Frazer are brothers. 5 Lizzie and Amy are sisters. 6 Lizzie and James are husband and wife. 7 Amy and Frazer are husband and wife. 8 Andrew and Ella are brother and sister. 9 Ella and Stephen are cousins. 10 Olivia and Anna are sisters.

2.1 2 a 3 b 4 e 5 f 6 d

2.2 2 is easy-going. 3 is happy 4 is sad 5 are hungry. 6 are thirsty.

2.3 2 is 3 isn't 4 are 5 is 6 is 7 are 8 is 9 are 10 is 11 are 12 is

2.4 2 He's 3 Is 4 isn't 5 are 6 They're 7 Where's 8 he 9 is 10 's

3.1 2 There's 3 There's 4 There are 5 There's 6 There are 7 There's 8 There's 9 There are 10 There are

3.2 2 there is 3 there is 4 there are 5 there isn't 6 there aren't

3.3 2 c 3 g 4 a 5 h 6 b 7 f 8 d

3.4 2 is 3 I'm 4 it's 5 there's 6 aren't 7 No 8 are 9 are 10 They're

4.1 2 a 3 a 4 a 5 b 6 b

4.2 2 a 3 f 4 e 5 c 6 b

4.3 2 That's 3 It's 4 That's 5 It's 6 That's 7 it's 8 That's 9 It's 10 That's

4.4 2 it's very upsetting to 3 because it's my mum's 4 it's OK by / with 5 it's good for me

R1.1 2 isn't 3 are 4 Is 5 No, 6 aren't 7 is 8 there is

R1.2 2 Am 3 are 4 is 5 Are / are 6 is 7 Is 8 am not

R1.3 2 All my relatives are lovely people. 3 Our step-father is thirty-three. 4 Are you bad-tempered in the mornings? 5 Aren't my cousin and I like each other? 6 You and Jolene are my best friends. 7 Is your grandfather a funny man? 8 Our parents aren't at work today.

R1.4 2 am 3 are 4 is 5 are 6 are 7 aren't 8 are 9 are 10 are 11 is

R1.5 2 Which girl is your sister? 3 Today is my mum and dad's wedding anniversary. 4 It's very kind of you to offer to help. 5 There are two bags full of shopping. 6 Aren't you late for the party? 7 How many children are there in your family? 8 There are the chocolate biscuits!

R1.6 2 isn't 3 He's 4 not 5 it's 6 is 7 There / Here 8 That's

R1.7 2 It's 3 that 4 it 5 It's 6 that's 7 it's

R1.8 1 is 2 It's 3 is 4 are 5 is 6 It's 7 are 8 I'm 9 there's 10 That's 11 there

5.1 2 have 3 have 4 has 5 has 6 have 7 have 8 has

5.2 2 haven't got 3 haven't got 4 hasn't got 5 hasn't got 6 haven't got 7 haven't got 8 hasn't got

5.3 2 Have Jason and his sister got big feet? No, they haven't. 3 Has Aunt Mabel got dyed hair? Yes, she has. 4 Have your sisters got bleached hair? Yes, they have. 5 Has Sophia got big eyes? No, she hasn't. 6 Has Ronaldo got a gorgeous smile? Yes, he has. 7 Have all the children in your family got long arms? No, they haven't. 8 Has Adam got spiky hair? No, he hasn't.

5.4 2 haven't 3 I've 4 got 5 have 6 has 7 have 8 We've 9 got 10 have

6.1 2 f 3 d 4 c 5 a 6 e

6.2 2 a 3 a 4 b 5 b 6 a

6.3 2 you've got 3 have 4 we've got 5 have 6 has got 7 I've got 8 don't have to 9 have

R2.1 2 Has, got 3 hasn't got 4 have got 5 Have, got 6 has, got 7 has got 8 Have, got

R2.2 2 We always have a great time at Sue's house. 3 Michelle has an amazing new hairstyle! 4 Does Noel have long hair these days? 5 Josie doesn't have a shower every day. 6 They have dinner late in Petra's family.

R2.3 2 Hilary has got blue eyes. 3 Hilary has got a big nose. 4 Nina has got long hair. 5 Nina hasn't got blue eyes. 6 Nina hasn't got a big nose.

3

Student's Book Answer Key

R2.4	2 a 3 f 4 e 5 c 6 b
R2.5	2 haven't got 3 have 4 don't have 5 have 6 haven't got 7 Has your brother got 8 has
R2.6	2 has 3 got 4 haven't 5 you've 6 I 7 got 8 we've 9 we've
R2.7	2 hasn't 3 got 4 haven't 5 has 6 got 7 have 8 have 9 haven't 10 got 11 have 12 have
R2.8	has got are Has got is Have you got have got are
7.1	2 b 3 b 4 a 5 a 6 b
7.2	2 make 3 watches 4 visit 5 wash 6 does 7 misses 8 play
7.3	2 Zena doesn't write e-mails at the weekend. 3 I don't wear scruffy clothes on Sundays. 4 Danny doesn't get up late on Sunday mornings. 5 They don't phone their friends on Saturdays and Sundays. 6 Gloria doesn't go away for the weekend.
7.4	2 loves 3 doesn't get 4 goes 5 makes 6 go 7 phones 8 invites 9 listen 10 talk 11 like 12 doesn't go 13 watches 14 does
8.1	2 f 3 e 4 a 5 d 6 b
8.2	2 Do your friends play computer games at the weekend? Yes, they do. 3 Do the boys kick a ball around in the park? No, they don't. 4 Does your mum go to town on Saturday afternoons? Yes, she does. 5 Does Simon's brother go skateboarding on Saturday mornings? No, he doesn't. 6 Do you meet your friends at the weekend? Yes, I do.
8.3	2 Why 3 does 4 Who 5 get 6 do
8.4	2 Doesn't Arthur spend his weekends at the bowling alley? 3 Doesn't Jackie stay in bed on Saturday mornings? 4 Doesn't Alex think Sunday evenings are boring? 5 Don't Kylie and her sister have a party most weekends? 6 Don't your parents listen to rap music? 7 Don't young people wear some great clothes?
9.1	2 Mum never makes breakfast on Saturdays. 3 Are you always lazy on Sundays? 4 They are often at home on Saturday evenings. 5 I rarely get up early on Sunday mornings. 6 Dad sometimes works at the weekend. 7 I'm never tired on Saturday nights. 8 Sonya usually goes out on Sundays.
9.2	2 every 3 twice 4 ever 5 Irene always 6 is usually 7 often does 8 times
9.3	2 Michelle and Grace make the dinner once a month. 3 Andrew sometimes sleeps all day on Sundays! 4 They go to the cinema twice a month. 5 The boys play football in the park every Sunday morning. 6 Teenagers are usually happy at weekends!
9.4	3 Giles usually surfs the Internet on Saturdays. 4 Geraldine sometimes surfs the Internet on Saturdays. 5 Giles never goes shopping with friends on Saturdays. 6 Geraldine always goes shopping with friends on Saturdays. 7 Giles rarely has a lie-in on Saturdays. 8 Geraldine often has a lie-in on Saturdays. 9 Giles never feels bored on Saturdays. 10 Geraldine rarely feels bored on Saturdays.
10.1	2 O 3 F 4 P 5 F 6 O 7 O 8 P
10.2	2 wants always: Samantha always wants to go out on Saturday evenings. 3 All night: Every night at ten o'clock, mum puts the cat out. 4 Ashley don't: Ashley doesn't help his mum with the housework. 5 They go usually: They usually go to the Internet café to go online. 6 a twice week: Dad does the shopping twice a week.
10.3	2 My mum doesn't like me going out on school nights. 3 What do you do on Saturday evenings? 4 I don't usually do anything special. 5 Yes, I do.
10.4	2 help 3 tidies 4 watch 5 don't play 6 takes 7 says 8 don't know 9 are 10 doesn't cook 11 get 12 sit 13 watches 14 watch 15 doesn't make
R3.1	2 goes 3 Does 4 think 5 you usually 6 often 7 puts 8 enjoy 9 doesn't 10 never surf
R3.2	2 goes 3 Do, chat 4 don't get up 5 cooks 6 Does, stay 7 doesn't wear 8 am never
R3.3	2 Judy always goes shopping on Saturdays. 3 Judy often eats lunch in town on Saturdays. 4 Judy never watches DVDs on Saturdays. 5 The twins sometimes get up early on Sundays. 6 The twins usually play football on Sundays. 7 The twins rarely meet Tom and Stef in town on Sundays. 8 The twins never stay up late on Sundays.
R3.4	2 don't 3 don't 4 doesn't 5 stays 6 watches 7 doesn't 8 rings 9 she's 10 visit

Rachel Finnie | Carol Frain | David A. Hill | Karen Thomas

TOP Grammar
From basic to upper-intermediate
Student's Book Answer Key

HELBLING LANGUAGES

TOP Grammar Student's Book Answer Key
by Rachel Finnie, Carol Frain, David A. Hill, Karen Thomas

© HELBLING LANGUAGES 2010
www.helblinglanguages.com

11 10 9 8 7 6 5
2016 2015 2014 2013 2012

All rights reserved; no part of this publication may be reproduced, stored in a retrieval system, or transmitted in any form or by any means, electronic, mechanical, photocopying, recording, or otherwise, without the prior written permission of the Publishers.

ISBN 978-3-85272-225-2

Project managed and edited by Paola Tite
Designed by BNC comunicazione
Printed by Athesia

Every effort has been made to trace the owners of any copyright material in this book. If notified, the publisher will be pleased to rectify any errors or omissions.

R3.5 2 plays 3 trains 4 goes 5 takes 6 does 7 watches 8 misses

R3.6 2 eat 3 stay 4 Does, work 5 play 6 get 7 don't go 8 do 9 does, wear 10 works

R3.7 is go get up have walk meet travel start finish don't go go play does doesn't like get watch listen comes go like don't drink Do

11.1 2 are 3 is 4 am 5 are 6 is 7 are 8 is

11.2 2 We're visiting some local ancient monuments. 3 Ron's learning how to juggle. 4 Be quiet! I'm trying to concentrate.

11.3 2 is learning 3 are dancing 4 are trying 5 are fishing 6 are going 7 am lying 8 is looking

11.4 2 is cooking 3 is watching 4 is putting 5 is having 6 is reading 7 are listening 8 is trying

12.1 2 Shane isn't writing his blog. 3 We aren't going to the cinema. 4 They aren't competing in the karate competition. 5 She isn't doing Sudoku puzzles. 6 Harry and Bob aren't skateboarding.

12.2 2 No, she isn't. 3 Yes, they are. 4 Yes, I am. 5 No, they aren't. 6 No, I'm not.

12.3 2 Where are 3 aren't 4 the boys 5 Isn't 6 What

12.4 2 Are you going to the drama group? 3 Is Ian reading in his room? 4 What are you doing? 5 Who is learning how to fly a kite? 6 Where are you going? 7 Why aren't they watching the match? 8 Aren't they playing in the band today?

12.5 2 e 3 b 4 c 5 a 6 f 7 h 8 d

13.1 2 next 3 always 4 summer 5 right 6 days 7 tomorrow 8 this

13.2 2 last month: They're studying English in London this month. 3 spending always: Angela's always spending her money on stupid things. 4 Learning you: Are you learning how to cook Chinese food? 5 Sophie and I am; Sophie and I are collecting flowers at the moment. 6 evening: What are you doing this evening?

13.3 2 At 12 o'clock on Saturday, we're having lunch in the hotel. 3 At 2 o'clock on Saturday, we're meeting at the sports centre. 4 At 3 o'clock on Saturday, we're taking part in the tournament. 5 At 7 o'clock on Saturday, we're going to a restaurant for dinner. 6 At 9 o'clock on Sunday, we're visiting the town. 7 At 12 o'clock on Sunday, we're leaving on the coaches.

13.4 2 They're 3 are 4 trying 5 is 6 are 7 listening 8 is 9 They're 10 writing 11 you're 12 spending

14.1 3 They usually spend their time surfing the Internet. 4 Sally and I are visiting Harlech Castle today. 5 You always make a mess when you paint! 6 ✔ 7 ✔ 8 I don't collect anything for a hobby.

14.2 2 d 3 a 4 f 5 b 6 e

14.3 2 I'm reading 3 You don't climb 4 I know 5 I'm saving up 6 I'm planning 7 isn't 8 interests 9 is learning 10 he's having 11 do you do 12 I sit

14.4 2 Are you enjoying 3 spends his free time 4 not giving up 5 Does your brother 6 They're all having 7 Bobby plays 8 We usually visit

15.1 2 do you do 3 hate 4 forgive 5 are seeing 6 eats 7 don't remember 8 am enjoying

15.2 2 John is thinking of buying some new rollerblades. 3 They don't understand how to write blogs. 4 Jason doesn't like walking the dog. 5 I think snowboarding is a dangerous hobby. 6 He doesn't believe I can rollerblade.

15.3 2 We're thinking: We think it's a great idea to take up juggling! 3 I enjoy: I'm enjoying this game a lot at the moment! 4 I'm knowing: I know how to look after tropical fish. 5 I'm not believing: I don't believe Stan does ballet in his free time! 6 I'm understanding: I understand all the rules of chess now.

15.4 2 b 3 a 4 b

R4.1 2 Do 3 not 4 is 5 having 6 Do you like 7 is thinking 8 dying

R4.2 2 Is, studying 3 am visiting 4 isn't listening 5 Are, collecting 6 Are, feeding 7 isn't making 8 Are, going

R4.3 2 c 3 f 4 h 5 a 6 g 7 e 8 b

R4.4 3 The cats are playing with a ball. 4 Mum and dad are watching television. 4 The dog is sleeping. 5 Granddad is juggling. 6 Grandma is painting a picture.

R4.5 2 like 3 surf 4 write 5 is staying 6 are showing 7 are walking 8 is taking 9 are having 10 thinks

Student's Book Answer Key

R4.6 2 usually have 3 are you having 4 want 5 are saying 6 do you think 7 is 8 are 9 don't like 10 keep 11 don't mind

R4.7 2 looks at 3 likes 4 serve 5 are making 6 wants 7 is giving 8 is looking for

R4.8 am having, am staying, go, don't swim, am sitting, are watching, are playing, is, are you doing, are you having fun, are you studying

A.1 2 A 3 D 4 C 5 A 6 D 7 C 8 B 9 D 10 B 11 A 12 B 13 D 14 B

A.2 2 sun isn't 3 are bored 4 There's 5 don't go

A.3 Student's own answers.

A.4 2 D 3 A 4 C 5 B 6 A 7 D 8 D 9 A 10 B

A.5 2 isn't 3 are 4 There's 5 are 6 There 7 are 8 aren't 9 are 10 there

A.6 2 He's 3 have 4 has 5 got 6 They've

16.1 2 were 3 was 4 were 5 was 6 were 7 were 8 was

16.2 2 The weather wasn't bad. 3 The staff at the airport weren't very helpful. 4 The travel agent wasn't busy. 5 They weren't in a self-catering apartment. 6 The sea wasn't rough. 7 The guided tour wasn't interesting. 8 The air stewards weren't friendly.

16.3 2 Were they tired at the end of the trip? No, they weren't. 3 Was your friend impressed by the sights? Yes, he/she was. 4 Was it a beautiful day? No, it wasn't. 5 Were the tourists annoyed about the delay? Yes, they were. 6 Were you pleased with the accommodation? No, I wasn't/we weren't. 7 Was the hotel room well-equipped? Yes, it was.

16.4 2 There was a baker's. 3 There were two policemen. 4 There was a café. 5 There weren't any firemen. 6 There wasn't a clothes shop.

17.1 2 smashed 3 talked 4 tried 5 stopped 6 changed 7 offered 8 stayed

17.2 b came c gave d left e saw f swam g took h told 2 The tour operator told passengers where to go. 3 I saw some amazing sights in London. 4 We swam in the sea despite the cold! 5 He came home from his business trip on Friday. 6 The tour guide gave us a lot of information about each place. 7 You took photos of the bridges and the canals. 8 The boat left early in the morning.

17.3 2 was 3 went 4 booked 5 set off 6 drove 7 left 8 checked in 9 found 10 had 11 sat 12 planned 13 wanted 14 were 15 landed 15 felt

18.1 2 We didn't have a good time on the voyage to Greece. 3 The travel agent didn't give us a brochure about the package deal. 4 The fare to New Zealand didn't cost a lot. 5 My friend didn't put us up at her place. 6 The passengers didn't think the airline was excellent. 7 I didn't enjoy the meal in the sushi bar.

18.2 2 Did your mum stay in a bed and breakfast? Yes, she did. 3 Did the customs officials explain everything? Yes, they did. 4 Did they find the tour of the capital interesting? No, they didn't. 5 Did you go surfing in Australia? Yes, I/we did. 6 Did the girls catch fish in the rock pools? No, they didn't. 7 Did he see an alligator in the Louisiana swamps? Yes, he did.

18.3 2 Joan remembered her passport. 3 Joan didn't give the taxi driver a tip. 4 Joan checked in at eight. 5 Joan didn't buy any perfume. 6 Joan didn't have a coffee at the airport. 7 Joan went through customs at nine. 8 Joan boarded the plane.

18.4 Student's own answers.

19.1 2 in 3 last 4 in 5 ago 6 at 7 last 8 ago

19.2 2 a 3 e 4 f 5 b 6 d

19.3 Correct order: 3, 5, 1, 4, 2

19.4 2 didn't have 3 booked 4 ate 5 gave 6 swim 7 swam 8 Did you go 9 They went 10 lost

R5.1 2 were 3 stopped 4 swam 5 see 6 did you live 7 last 8 did 9 buy 10 ago

R5.2 2 read 3 regretted 4 didn't see 5 Did, get 6 made 7 didn't take 8 felt 9 was 10 didn't think

R5.3 2 What did you see in London? 3 How did you travel to London? 4 Did you stay in a hotel? 5 What did you enjoy most about London? 6 When did you come home? 7 Did you have a good journey home?
2 b 3 a 4 c 5 d 6 f 7 g

R5.4 2 lived 3 ran 4 went 5 was 6 became 7 could 8 had 9 came 10 talked 11 liked 12 was 13 were 14 played

R5.5 2 was 3 hurt 4 couldn't 5 didn't go 6 went 7 Did, get on 8 were 9 kept 10 was

R5.6 2 Did you drink beer? 3 Did you have a good time? 4 Did you talk to anyone? 5 What did they say to you?

20.1 3 Molly and I used to enjoy watching baseball. 4 ✔ 5 You didn't use to watch cricket, but you do now. 6 Henry used to play team sports more than he does now. 7 ✔ 8 Their dad used to win every boxing match. 9 I used to think that rugby was great to watch. 10 ✔

20.2 2 used 3 use 4 used 5 use 6 use 7 didn't 8 didn't

20.3 2 Nell used to ride her bike every day. 3 Bryan didn't use to like volleyball. 4 I used to own an expensive cricket bat. 5 Did you use to go skiing every winter? 6 My parents didn't use to watch sports on TV. 7 Did your dad use to be a famous athlete? 8 Did she use to play in the tennis tournament?

20.4 2 to be 3 use 4 used 5 to be 6 used 7 use 8 use

21.1 2 was 3 were 4 was 5 were 6 was 7 were 8 was

21.2 2 were waiting 3 weren't listening 4 were getting 5 wasn't enjoying 6 wasn't running 7 wasn't paying 8 was wearing

21.3 2 Were you playing snooker? Yes, I was. 3 Were the people in the crowd supporting the national champion? Yes, they were. 4 Was Harry going scuba diving? Yes, he was. 5 Were the girls playing rounders? No, they weren't. 6 Were the judges smiling? No, they weren't. 7 Was the trainer giving him a telling-off? No, he wasn't.

21.4 2 was playing 3 Was your 4 wasn't 5 was working 6 Were all 7 were 8 weren't making 9 was

22.1 2 shouting 3 was working 4 Did you enjoy 5 turned up 6 stopped 7 was listening 8 Were you doing

22.2 2 while 3 when 4 while 5 when 6 while 7 while 8 while

22.3 2 was running 3 rang 4 were, doing 5 were painting 6 broke 7 scored 8 was getting

22.4 2 was getting: I was watching a football match on TV when dad got home from work. 3 Were you play: Were you playing golf when it started to rain? 4 I was to jogging: I was jogging through the park at nine this morning. 5 didn't playing: Dan didn't play volleyball that afternoon. 6 Eleanor and Gemma exercising: Eleanor and Gemma were exercising at the gym all morning. 7 The children was diving: The children were diving from a low diving board into the pool. 8 We watched: We were watching the cricket on TV when there was a power cut.

R6.1 2 used 3 was 4 Did 5 to think 6 Was 7 Were you having 8 while 9 started 10 were already sleeping

R6.2 2 The football trainer was talking to his team. 3 Some people were watching the sports events. 4 A girl was jumping. 5 Some kids were having a drink of water. 6 Some kids were running in a race. 7 Some parents were shouting. 8 Some kids were eating oranges.

R6.3 2 were having 3 was showing 4 watched 5 asked 6 was getting 7 started 9 didn't get

R6.4 2 was doing 3 was staring 4 was lifting 5 didn't see 6 went 7 was putting on 8 thought/was thinking 9 made 10 returned 11 walked 12 kissed 13 looked 14 was wearing 15 was trying 16 was happening 17 started 18 introduced

R6.5 2 A 3 C 4 B 5 C 6 B 7 B 8 C 9 C 10 A

B.1 2 A 3 C 4 C 5 B 6 D 7 A 8 D 9 B 10 D 11 A 12 D 13 A

B.2 2 to be 3 were there 4 was bad 5 wasn't warm

B.3 Student's own answers.

B.4 2 A 3 C 4 D 5 A 6 C 7 C 8 B 9 D 10 C 11 C 12 A 13 D 14 B 15 B

B.5 2 didn't 3 were 4 was 5 was 6 not 7 did 8 diving 9 were 10 when 11 did 12 were 13 while 14 when 15 didn't

23.1 2 done I 3 drunk I 4 given I 5 made I 6 moved R 7 put I 8 sat I 9 visited R 10 written I 11 shown I 12 wanted R 13 arrived R 14 bought I 15 hired R 16 eaten I 17 played R 18 sung I 19 walked R 20 washed R

23.2 1 rented 2 broken 3 stolen 4 fallen 5 hidden 6 spoken 7 cut 8 lost

Student's Book Answer Key

23.3 1 relaxed 2 bored 3 interesting 4 tiring 5 excited 6 pleased 7 terrifying 8 amazed

23.4 2 ✔ 3 It's no good crying over spilt milk! 4 We felt frozen and wondered when she was going to turn the central heating on. 5 6 You can't get money back that's spent. 7 8 The kids were really scared when they watched that horror movie.

24.1 2 have 3 has 4 have 5 have 6 have 7 has 8 have

24.2 2 has redecorated 3 have seen 4 have planted 5 have gone 6 has visited

24.3 2 Have Dave and Ryan repaired the hole in the roof? Yes, they have. 3 Has Henry used the gardening tools we gave him? Yes, he has. 4 Have the builders finished the work in the attic? No, they haven't.

24.4 2 Are you washed: Have you washed the kitchen floor yet? 3 Has Candice moves: Has Candice moved to her new flat? 4 have they build: Where have they built their new house? 5 are living: Olga's grandparents have lived in that cottage all their lives. 6 I not finished: Sorry mum, I haven't finished the housework.

24.5 2 has, done 3 has made 4 has washed 5 has, swept 6 has tidied 7 has hung 8 has cooked 9 has cleaned 10 has put 11 hasn't eaten 12 has forgotten

25.1 2 They have just moved into their new home. 3 The kids have just arrived at the youth hostel. 4 The electrician has just repaired our washing machine. 5 The electricity has just gone off. 6 The last party guests have just left.

25.2 2 already 3 already 4 already 5 yet 6 still 7 still 8 already

25.3 2 just 3 already 4 yet 5 just 6 already 7 already 8 still

25.4 2 f 3 a 4 c 5 d 6 b

25.5 2 yet 3 already 4 already 5 just 6 yet 7 already 8 yet

26.1 2 b 3 a 4 a 5 a 6 a

26.2 2 never 3 ever 4 never 5 never 6 ever 7 never 8 never

26.3 2 Leo and Bob have never stayed in a youth hostel. 3 Have you ever looked in the attic? 4 Has Nigella ever invited you to her house? 5 Iris has never been able to afford a mortgage. 6 The landlord has never put up my rent. 7 Have you ever wondered who lives in that mansion? 8 Jeremy has never used the central heating.

26.4 2 you ever done 3 I have 4 I've never 5 never 6 ever

27.1 2 b 3 a 4 a 5 b 6 b

27.2 2 haven't lived 3 for 4 since 5 for 6 have been

27.3 2 since 3 I've known 4 for 5 did you 6 I haven't 7 spoken 8 you've

27.4 2 since I saw 3 have known Eric 4 since they decorated 5 have you had

28.1 2 a 3 f 4 b 5 c 6 e

28.2 2 b 3 a 4 b 5 b

28.3 2 haven't seen 3 has, swept 4 built 5 did, move 6 have, lived 7 Have, paid 8 has, had

28.4 2 haven't heard 3 happened 4 they've won 5 won 6 they moved 7 yet 8 haven't finished 9 yet 10 chose 11 yesterday 12 did they hear 13 They've been

R7.1 2 haven't been 3 Has 4 decided 5 already 6 seen 7 ever 8 never

R7.2 2 has, worked 3 haven't spent 4 has put 5 haven't spoken 6 has bought 7 has wanted 8 Have, been

R7.3 2 Ten years ago, Josh never made a meal. Recently he has learnt to cook. 3 Ten years ago, Josh shared a bedroom with his brother. Recently he has moved to his own bedsit. 4 Ten years ago, Josh was at school. Recently he has got a job as an interior designer. 5 Ten years ago, Emma only ate vegetables. Recently she has started eating meat. 6 Ten years ago, Emma hated gardening. Recently she has planted some bulbs and flowers. 7 Ten years ago, Emma lived with her parents. Recently she has moved to her own flat.

R7.4 2 has 3 has 4 have 5 he's 6 never 7 Have 8 ever 9 has 10 He's 11 have 12 since 13 has 14 yet

R7.5 2 has just gone 3 Have you ever been 4 has bought 5 Has Charles ever seen 6 have always loved

R7.6 2 was 3 Have you had 4 didn't get up 5 was 6 Did you see 7 have always liked 8 moved, have lived

8

R7.7 2 C 3 B 4 B 5 C 6 B 7 C 8 B

29.1 3 You have been listening to a lecture about science. 4 Susan has been doing her homework all evening. 5 ✔ 6 ✔ 7 The girls have been playing netball in the playground. 8 Tina has been taking part in some extra drama classes.

29.2 2 haven't been looking at 3 haven't been waiting 4 has been going on 5 has been choosing 6 haven't been studying 7 has been thinking 8 have been decorating

29.3 2 Has the head teacher been preparing the new timetable? No, he/she hasn't. 3 Has your English teacher been marking the exams? Yes, he/she has. 4 Has Simon been having a PE lesson? No, he hasn't. 5 Has your mum been attending pottery classes at night school? Yes, she has. 6 Have the children been writing on the board? No, they haven't.

29.4 2 They've been listening to CDs from a French course. 3 She's been reading essays by children in her class. 4 He's been learning to drive for a very long time. 5 They've been playing in a rock band since they were at college. 6 They've been having swimming lessons all morning.

30.1 2 has been reading 3 finished 4 been trying 5 been taking 6 gone 7 been playing 8 been doing

30.2 2 has left 3 has been studying 4 Has, been doing 5 haven't been attending 6 have, been taking 7 haven't decided 8 Has, marked

30.3 2 e 3 a 4 f 5 b 6 g 7 h 8 d

30.4 2 Mal and Trevor have been working on the computer. They have learnt how to send e-mails. 3 My friends have been sitting at their desks. They have written an essay. 4 The students have been reading their history books. They have revised things for their exams. 5 My mum has been talking to a night-school tutor. She has agreed to enrol for IT classes. 6 I have been thinking about English grammar. I have done this exercise.

31.1 2 had finished 3 hadn't gone over 4 had started 5 hadn't finished 6 Had, put away 7 had learnt 8 had done

31.2 2 had finished 3 had read 4 had closed 5 had taught 6 hadn't noticed 7 had prepared 8 had passed

31.3 2 e 3 a 4 f 5 c 6 d

31.4 2 hadn't 3 sat 4 hadn't 5 finished 6 Hadn't 7 remembered 8 forgotten

31.5 2 I hadn't realised ancient Greek was so interesting! 3 Had you heard about the extra lessons? 4 The teacher had written the results on the board. 5 My parents had enrolled for an IT class at night school. 6 The school had changed a lot since I went there. 7 Everyone had finished writing their essay. 8 Millie had attended two different high schools in America.

32.1 2 b 3 a 4 a 5 b 6 b

32.2 1 started 2 had you studied 3 hadn't started 4 had 5 knew 6 didn't get

32.3 2 Jessie had studied at junior school before she went to grammar school. 3 The students went out after they had finished their projects. 4 The teachers had had a meeting before lessons started. 5 I arrived at school after the science lesson had started. 6 I had studied for hours in the evening before I took the English test. 7 Jenny met her friend and walked to college after she had eaten her breakfast. 8 The teacher gave us an unexpected geography test after we had had a half-hour break.

33.1 2 had 3 waiting 4 had been 5 learning 5 They'd 7 had 8 been hoping

33.2 2 had been thinking 3 had been teaching 4 had been learning 5 had been studying 6 hadn't been waiting

33.3 2 Miss Brown had been marking tests. 3 Some children had been chatting in their classroom. 4 It had been raining heavily. 5 The head teacher had been looking at the new curriculum. 6 The PE teacher had been planning extra lessons.

33.4 1 No 2 been, had 3 they, hadn't 4 Had, had

33.5 2 had been reading to us for half an hour. 3 had been writing my essay for one hour. 4 had been doing her homework for three hours. 5 had been learning Spanish for four years.

R8.1 2 been 3 doing 4 had 5 Hadn't 6 when 7 all 8 hadn't

R8.2 2 went 3 visited 4 had talked 5 knew 6 had 7 walked 8 knew 9 had worried 10 got

Student's Book Answer Key

R8.3 2 Had Michaela and Josie been rehearsing for the school play? No, they hadn't. 3 Had Professor Robert Parker been preparing the curriculum? Yes, he had. 4 Had the students been having extra lessons in science? Yes, they had. 5 Had Ursula been planning to apply to Oxford University? Yes, she had. 6 Had you been studying for the maths test? No, I hadn't. 7 Had Sophie and Leila been waiting for their exam results? Yes, they had. 8 Had it been snowing since the weekend? No, it hadn't.

R8.4 2 had asked 3 Had, been waiting 4 hadn't thought/hadn't been thinking 5 had been 6 had been working 7 had lost 8 had enjoyed

R8.5 2 A 3 C 4 B 5 A 6 C 7 A 8 B 9 A 10 C 11 B

R8.6 2 have been learning 3 has been living, got 4 has been working 5 hasn't come, quarrelled 6 had been talking, opened, walked 7 have been having, have been discussing, haven't finished 8 had just finished, started

C.1 2 A 3 D 4 B 5 A 6 C 7 B 8 D 9 A 10 B 11 C 12 B

C.2 2 has been teaching 3 had done/had finished 4 had been 5 had helped

C.3 Student's own answers.

C.4 2 Yes 3 visited/seen 4 haven't 5 he's 6 has 7 He's 8 planted 9 has 10 got

C.5 2 secondary 3 prospectus 4 application 5 qualification

C.6 2 have already made my bed 3 hasn't yet 4 have already read 5 hasn't moved into 6 have just seen

34.1 2 aren't going to apply 3 am going to try 4 are going to have 5 isn't going to work 6 are going to go 7 isn't going to stay 8 is going to come 9 isn't going to be 10 am going to like

34.2 2 Are your colleagues going to organise a surprise party for the boss? No, they aren't. 3 Are you going to apply for promotion next year? Yes, I am. 4 Is Sara going to take over the job of manageress? Yes, she is. 5 Am I going to get my Christmas bonus this month? No, you aren't. 6 Are they going to move to offices closer to the city centre? No, they aren't.

34.3 2 am going to ask 3 am going to tell 4 isn't going to do 5 aren't going to change 6 are, going to take

34.4 2 are going to offer 3 Are you going to move 4 are going to employ 5 aren't going to get 6 'm not going to retire 7 are going to advertise 8 is going to interview

35.1 2 The manager will see you soon. 3 He will be busy all summer. 4 Will they advertise the jobs in the newspaper? 5 I'm sure Grace will get the promotion. 6 Will they pay you a good salary? 7 I hope you will enjoy the work. 8 Do you think I will do well at the interview?

35.2 2 The doctor won't have time to see you later. 3 The pay for that IT job won't be very high. 4 Elizabeth won't get a qualification in medicine. 5 The electrician won't charge a lot for his work. 6 We won't get a good pension when we retire.

35.3 2 a 3 f 4 c 5 e 6 d

35.4 2 Will there be any vacancies here soon? Yes, there will. 3 Will he feel nervous at the interview? No, he won't. 4 Will you catch up on your work before the weekend? Yes, I will. 5 Will they expect me to work at weekends? No, they won't. 6 Will Roseanne earn enough to live on? No, she won't.

36.1 2 ✔ 3 ✔ 4 The committee will probably promote Mr Taylor to managing director. 5 ✔ 6 ✔ 7 I'll talk to you later – I'm at work at the moment. 8 His secretary won't retire for another ten years. 9 I hope you'll be happy in your new job. 10 ✔

36.2 2 will be 3 start 4 probably 5 wonder 6 hope 7 will 8 soon

36.3 2 c 3 b 4 g 5 f 6 a 7 h 8 d

36.4 2 Norman get: I expect Norman will get the job. 3 won't think: I don't think you'll find part-time work here. 4 will like: I like my job but I'll look for something different in the future. 5 will hope: I hope my new employer will be nice! 6 Will have you: Will you have time to do a full-time job and run the house?

37.1 2 will help 3 Will, have 4 will show 5 won't do 6 will, buy 7 won't take 8 will pay

37.2 2 will miss 3 will have 4 won't work 5 Will, post 6 will show 7 won't listen 8 Will, close

37.3 2 a 3 f 4 e 5 c 6 b

37.4 2 I'll buy you a cake. 3 I'll help you find your diary. 4 I'll have a salad, please. 5 I'll pay for the drinks. 6 Will you close the window, please?

R9.1 2 is going 3 to ask 4 I'll 5 probably 6 tell 7 you'll be 8 you're going

R9.2 2 Jenny's going to have a lie-in. 3 Jenny's going to catch up on work. 4 Jenny's going to cook supper for her work colleagues. 5 Jenny's going to study the company reports.

R9.3 2 I will have to take over some of his work. 3 I will use his desk and answer his phone. 4 I will get paid overtime. 5 My boss will oversee my performance.

R9.4 2 No, he won't. 3 Yes, he will. 4 No, she isn't. 5 Yes, she is. 6 No, he won't.

R9.5 2 will 3 to 4 won't 5 are 6 be

R9.6 2 are going to 3 will be 4 is going 5 earn 6 will charge 7 will go 8 will get

R9.7 2 will demolish 3 will, get ahead 4 are, going to do 5 will take 6 is going to take over 7 are going to advertise 8 will get

R9.8 2 am going to go 3 am going to attend 4 are you going to stay 5 will stay 6 are you going to leave 7 will leave 8 am going to work 9 am going to work 10 will send

38.1 4, 6, 7, 9

38.2 2 am seeing 3 are you doing 4 is spending 5 leaves 6 is going 7 arrive 8 starts

38.3 2 leaves 3 is taking 4 is going 5 starts 6 are having 7 am leaving, leaves 8 arrives

38.4 2 I am going to the clinic for an injection tomorrow. 3 I am not seeing the heart specialist this week. 4 We are visiting grandma in hospital tomorrow. 5 The doctor is seeing her in two weeks' time. 6 My physiotherapy session starts at two tomorrow.

39.1 2 I'll ask 3 will 4 'm going to 5 I'm going to 6 Are you going to

39.2 3 I have: I'm hungry. I think I'll have a bacon sandwich. 4 ✔ 5 you're feeling: I'm sure you'll feel better soon. 6 ✔

39.3 2 Stay still! This injection won't hurt at all! 3 My appointment is at 9 a.m. tomorrow. I am having an X-ray on my ankle. 4 Your temperature will probably go up after the operation. 5 Elsie says she is a lot better and she isn't going to stay in bed for another minute. 6 The doctor doesn't know what to say. So I am seeing a specialist next week.

39.4 2 won't feel/isn't going to feel 3 won't be 4 are going to invite 5 will be 6 will invite 7 will be 8 are sending/are going to send 9 'll ask 10 will write 11 will go/am going

39.5 2 I'll go 3 starts 4 don't go 5 Are you taking 6 taking 7 I'll 8 I'm

40.1 2 will be coming round 3 will be doing 4 Will, be working 5 won't be eating 6 will be hurting

40.2 2 will have recovered 3 will have disappeared 4 will have left 5 will have diagnosed 6 Will, have started

40.3 2 have used 3 be treating 4 be examining 5 have taken 6 be feeling

40.4 2 b 3 e 4 a 5 f 6 c

40.5 2 be working 3 won't have finished 4 won't be 5 be looking 6 will have 7 have made 8 will be eating

R10.1 2 will close 3 will have gone 4 am having 5 will be starting 6 I'll do 7 will have finished 8 you're going to need

R10.2 2 The doctor starts his rounds at nine. 3 They are going to operate on Billie's leg. 4 Your anaesthetic will have worn off by this evening. 5 All the patients will be having physiotherapy at four. 6 This tablet will help your headache to go. 7 I am going to the dentist at nine tomorrow. 8 John will have finished his therapy soon.

R10.3 2 having opened: Will the chemist have opened by ten? 3 sees: The optician will see me at eleven tomorrow. 4 will do: By ten tomorrow morning, Mitch will have done his medical exams. 5 going be: Mum, I think Ollie's going to be sick! 6 will to stop: I hope my tooth will stop hurting very soon!

R10.4 2 have 3 by 4 be 5 will 6 be

R10.5 2 will 3 will be able 4 will have 5 'm going 6 is seeing

R10.6 2 don't read, won't be able to write 3 arrives, will tell 4 breaks down, will call 5 is, will buy 6 is, will go

R10.7 2 are having, are going to talk 3 will recover, will take 4 won't eat 5 is going to feel

D.1 2 C 3 B 4 A 5 B 6 D 7 B 8 A 9 D 10 C

11

Student's Book Answer Key

D.2 2 will be 3 won't 4 have got 5 doesn't

D.3 2 A 3 D 4 D 5 A 6 B 7 D 8 C 9 C 10 B 11 A 12 C

D.4 2 are 3 to 4 see 5 probably 6 won't 7 suffer 8 will 9 going 10 aren't 11 see

D.5 2 going to have a party 3 am seeing the doctor 4 finishes in 5 has been suffering 6 can be

41.1 3, 6, 7, 9, 10

41.2 2 do 3 Don't 4 have 5 go 6 look 7 don't 8 will

41.3 2 Let's ask for a refund. 3 Think carefully before you buy it! 4 Don't forget to bring your money! 5 Don't stand in the doorway! 6 Go to the back of the queue! 7 Let's go for a coffee. 8 Meet me outside the bank, will you?

41.4 2 a 3 f 4 e 5 c 6 b

41.5 Possible answers: 2 Let's get a takeaway / go to the restaurant. 3 Let's meet up at the Verdi café later. 4 Let's have a party. 5 Let's go to the shopping centre. 6 Let's go to the cinema.

42.1 2 to 3 to go 4 learn 5 to study 6 to get 7 have left 8 to phone 9 be working 10 look

42.2 2 to wash 3 to learn 4 to ask 5 to be 6 to wear 7 to go 8 to get

42.3 2 He hopes not to lose his job at the end of the summer. 3 Please tell him not to forget his passport. 4 Simon hopes not to fail his driving test again. 5 I must remember not to call Miss Lee by her first name! 6 We hope not to find the house in a mess after the party!

42.4 2 f 3 e 4 b 5 a 6 d

42.5 2 to go 3 to get 4 to need 5 to buy 6 to be

43.1 2 G 3 P 4 A 5 S 6 P

43.2 2 going 3 losing 4 selling 5 changing 6 building

43.3 2 d 3 b 4 f 5 e 6 a

43.4 2 writing 3 reading 4 writing 5 thinking 6 telling 7 doing

43.5 2 shopping 3 buying 4 sitting 5 doing 6 to walk 7 avoiding 8 getting 9 ordering 10 spending 11 to buy

44.1 2 Nancy decided to open a bank account. 3 Mum prefers to shop at the local grocer's. 4 Shall I help you to carry this bag? 5 Are you able to pay by cash? 6 The sales assistant refused to help me.

44.2 2 are planning 3 Remember 4 expect 5 refused 6 hope 7 wants 8 doesn't know

44.3 2 c 3 f 4 e 5 d 6 a

44.4 2 have to pay 3 to send 4 forget to do 5 to arrange 6 to pay bills 7 to see 8 remember to let 8 to order

45.1 2 coming 3 pushing 4 to tell 5 swimming 6 to know 7 to catch 8 buying 9 working 10 to spend

45.2 2 d 3 a 4 c 5 f 6 e

45.3 2 to get 3 to open 4 to give 5 shopping 6 spending 7 buying 8 having 9 to write

45.4 2 a 3 b 4 a 5 a 6 a 7 a, b

46.1 2 about 3 apart from/except for 4 without 5 at 6 of 7 on 8 for

46.2 2 good 3 wasting 4 having 5 of 6 saying 7 with 8 like

46.3 2 taking 3 paying 4 resting 5 asking 6 buying 7 shopping 8 doing

46.4 2 c 3 a 4 d 5 f 6 e

46.5 2 for to clean: Look! Dad's got a new gadget for cleaning the car. 3 without pay: I'm afraid we think you walked out without paying. 4 After say: After saying his goodbyes, the manager left to start his retirement. 5 fond to look: I'm very fond of looking at street markets. 6 to tidy: I haven't got round to tidying my wardrobe yet!

R11.1 2 Don't 3 Call 4 look 5 to go 6 buying 7 have spent 8 shopping 9 looking 10 with

R11.2 2 say 3 wearing 4 seeing 5 say 6 to want 7 agree

R11.3 2 get 3 agreeing 4 catching 5 look 6 saving 7 opening 8 to find

R11.4 2 going 3 listening 4 to save 5 to take 6 to bring 7 to shop/shopping 8 thinking/ talking

R11.5 2 going to dance: We enjoy going dancing every weekend. 3 Sitting there: Sit there and wait for me, please! 4 wants opening: Ellen wants to open her own music store one day. 5 the change rooms: I think I left my bag in the changing rooms. 6 to be: Bob isn't used to being a sales assistant.

R11.6 2 putting 3 say 4 wait 5 seeing 6 to raise

R11.7 2 to pay 3 to see 4 to bring 5 trying 6 lingering/linger 7 taking 8 to sort out

R11.8 2 What about going to the cinema tonight? 3 ✔ 4 Why did you stop painting? 5 I'm sorry, it's too late to enter the competition. 6 ✔ 7 Can you help me to carry the luggage, please? 8 I'll never forget travelling round India when I was a young child.

R11.9 2 wandering 3 to buy 4 realising 5 shopping 6 going 7 to borrow 8 spending 9 having

E1 2 A 3 C 4 C 5 A 6 D 7 B 8 A 9 C 10 B 11 A 12 A 13 D

E2 2 of shopping 3 leaving 4 ironing 5 play 6 remember to take

E3 Student's own answers.

E4 2 go 3 do 4 to 5 other 6 with 7 stop 8 to 9 staying 10 go 11 see/visit 12 forward 13 doing

E5 2 millionaires 3 investments 4 inflation 5 bankrupt 6 extremely 7 spending 8 financial 9 payments 10 economical

E6 2 without saying 3 felt like crying 4 can't help buying 5 worth raising 6 Before going away 7 very good at 8 not old enough

47.1 2 I can come to your birthday party tomorrow. 3 She can't finish the work until Friday. 4 I'm so hungry I could eat a horse! 5 Mike couldn't go to Jane's wedding because he was busy. 6 Can you come to the fireworks with us tonight? 7 When could they help to prepare the decorations?

47.2 2 they can 3 she couldn't 4 he could 5 I could 6 we can't

47.3 2 Do you can: Can you 3 she cans: she can 4 Could they to go: Could they go 5 can't: We couldn't visit the folk dance festival yesterday. 6 didn't can: couldn't

47.4 2 d 3 f 4 b 5 c 6 e

47.5 2 I couldn't go to the garden party because it was raining. 3 We were asking him if he could come to the dance. 4 I didn't play the violin, but I could play the guitar. 5 He said he could sing very well. 6 You couldn't play loud music there after midnight.

48.1 2 Steve can't arrange the party room next Saturday. 3 Susan couldn't finish preparing the party food last night. 4 I can't go dancing tomorrow because of my bad leg. 5 Dan couldn't put up the Christmas tree last night because he was very tired.

48.2 2 Could I have a plate of chips, please? 3 Can I borrow your red pen, please? 4 Could you (possibly) lend me 20 euros, please? 5 Could you bring me a pizza Napoli, please?

48.3 2 Mike couldn't speak English when he started school, but he can now. 3 Jane couldn't cook when she went to university, but she can now. 4 They couldn't play tennis when they started lessons, but they can now. 5 I couldn't swim when I went to the seaside, but I can now.

48.4 2 He wasn't able to go to the school fête last week. He had a cold. 3 I didn't manage to see the exhibition yet. I was out of town. 4 I wasn't allowed to park my car in front of the restaurant. It's private. 5 I'm sorry, sir, but you aren't permitted to smoke inside this building.

48.5 2 Can I carry your bag for you? 3 Can I make you a cup of coffee, Dad? 4 Can I take your books back to the library?

49.1 2 I may go to the club dinner tonight. 3 Susan might not visit the Edinburgh Festival. 4 Nadal may not win Wimbledon next year. 5 My father may have a retirement party. 6 I might not pass my maths exam.

49.2 2 Maybe he'll come with us to the New Year's Dance. 3 Perhaps Chelsea will win the Champions League. 4 Maybe they'll invite us to their engagement party. 5 Perhaps she'll go to the Easter Races without you. 6 Maybe we'll put up the Christmas decorations tonight.

49.3 2 May I use your barbecue for my garden party, Mrs Roberts? 3 You may sit down now the speeches have finished. 4 Please may I/we open my/our birthday presents? 5 May I ask you a question, please?

13

Student's Book Answer Key

R12.1 2 can't 3 can't 4 could 5 can't 6 couldn't 7 couldn't 8 can/could 9 Can/Could 10 can/could 11 can/could

R12.2 2 Could you tell me what time it is, please? 3 Can I go to Liz's party please, mum? 4 Can you help me arrange the party room, please? 5 Could I leave school an hour earlier today, please? 6 Could you take me to the station, please?

R12.3 2 Can, play 3 couldn't come 4 can speak 5 Could, help 6 can't go

R12.4 2 can 3 could 4 couldn't 5 could 6 could 7 can't 8 can 9 could

R12.5 2 will be able to 3 are allowed to 4 will be able to 5 are not allowed to 6 won't be able to

R12.6 2 I may/might go to the Lord Mayor's Parade on Saturday. 3 My dad might give me the money I need. 4 They might not be able to find the way to the Festival. 5 She may/might marry Paul after all. 6 We might finish the firework display before it rains.

R12.7 2 May I have another piece of Christmas cake, please? 3 You may go home when you've decorated the room. 4 You may not open your presents yet. 5 May I clean the party room now, please? 6 May I sit next to Suzanne at dinner, please?

50.1 2 You must cross the road at the zebra crossing. 3 You must not walk on the grass. 4 You must not smoke inside the restaurant. 5 You must wear a seat-belt when you drive. 6 You must not go out without your identity card.

50.2 2 must not 3 must not 4 must 5 must 6 must not

50.3 2 'Must Sue come in the car with us?' 3 'Must we all watch *The Lion King* tonight?' 4 'Must Jimmy play football with us?' 5 'Must Aunt Jane take me to the seaside?' 6 'Must Jack finish his maths before he can play?'

50.4 3 You must go to the next Chelsea match with me. 4 It must be lunchtime because I'm hungry/I haven't eaten since breakfast. 5 You mustn't park your car here because it's private. 6 He must be that boy's father because he looks like him.

50.5 2 must have been 3 must have been 4 must have had 5 must have left/set off /got up 6 must have cost

51.1 2 She has to feed her pet rabbit every morning. 3 We don't have to go to school tomorrow because it's a holiday. 4 He doesn't have to be there until four o'clock. 5 You have to tidy your room before you go out. 6 They don't have to finish their homework now; they can do it later.

51.2 2 Has she got to come to our party? 3 Does he have to go to the police station? 4 Have we got to study the American penal system? 5 Do you have to visit them tonight? 6 Have they got to stay with us all week?

51.3 2 b 3 a 4 a 5 b 6 a

51.4 2 personal 3 external 4 personal 5 personal 6 external 7 external 8 external

52.1 2 need to 3 needs to 4 doesn't need to 5 need to 6 don't need to

52.2 2 don't need to visit 3 doesn't need to come 4 needn't finish 5 needn't pay 6 doesn't need to worry

52.3 need to 2 Do, need to 3 Need 4 Need 5 Does, need to 6 Need

52.4 2 she had to train twice a week to stay in the team. 3 will have to prepare everything for the party ourselves. 4 Will she have to bring her guitar to the party? 5 did you have to go to school on Saturdays?

52.5 2 I don't think you need to pay for it now. 3 He didn't have to go there every day. 4 All schools will be obliged to enforce the new regulations. 5 The kitchen needs tidying. 6 You needn't worry about me.

R13.1 2 must, mustn't 3 must, don't have to 4 mustn't, must 5 must, mustn't 6 must, mustn't

R13.2 2 Have they got to come to the station with us? 3 Have you got to leave your books all over the floor? 4 Has she got to work so late at night? 5 Have we got to finish the project by Friday? 6 Has he got to keep playing that computer game?

R13.3 2 mustn't to drive: You mustn't drive so fast on this road. 3 didn't must: They didn't have to come here until later. 4 Do I must: Do I have to/Must I tidy my bedroom now? 5 Does he has to: Does he have to work on Friday? 6 haven't to: They don't have to buy them now.

R13.4 Student's own answers.

R13.5 2 need 3 must 4 need/have 5 mustn't 6 need/have 7 must 8 have/need 9 have/need 10 have/need

R13.6 2 d 3 f 4 c 5 a 6 e

R13.7 2 We didn't need to/have to get the train last night. Mum gave us a lift. 3 You needn't/don't have to run to run, Jane. The train's already left! 4 ✔ 5 You mustn't use your mobile phone during the flight. 6 ✔

53.1 2 Shall I catch the bus if they clear the snow? 3 Shall we come if it doesn't rain? 4 Shall I buy some winter clothes tomorrow? 5 Shall we go to the beach if the weather changes? 6 Shall I bring you some boots for when it snows?

53.2 2 When shall we get there? 3 Which coat shall I wear? 4 How shall we get to your house? 5 Who shall I ask to go to the dance with me? 6 Where shall we meet you?

53.3 2 When should we tell him about the problem? 3 Should we bring our sports clothes with us? 4 What should I say when I meet him? 5 Should I ask her to lend me the money? 6 Where should we wait for you if it rains?

53.4 2 You shouldn't get to work late, Linda. 3 You should take more exercise, Jimmy. 5 Driving should be easier now. 6 The slopes should be good for skiing/covered in snow now.

54.1 2 He had better work harder. 3 She had better be more careful. 4 They ought to finish the work quickly or the boss will tell them off. 5 You had better ask someone to help you or you'll never be able to hand in your project on time. 6 We ought to go and see this film tomorrow.

54.2 2 He ought not to go out in this thunderstorm. 3 You had better not use your car so much in town. 4 She ought not to stay out so late at night. 5 We had better not speak to them until we decide.

54.3 2 Lucy's so intelligent she's bound to pass all her exams. 3 Jeremy's flight is due to land at four o'clock. 4 The train is due (here) in five minutes. 5 Manchester United is such a strong team that it's bound to win the cup again this year.

54.4 2 due 3 bound 4 oughtn't 5 had better

55.1 2 Will you visit the art exhibition with me, Judy? 3 Will you watch the football match with me, Danny? 4 Will you eat at the Indian restaurant with me, Helen? 5 Will you come to the firework display with me, Bill? 6 Will you fly to Sardinia with me, Avril?

55.2 2 Would you give me your credit card, please? 3 Would you wait in the queue, please? 4 Would you open your suitcase, please? 5 Would you fasten your seat-belt, please? 6 Would you sign at the bottom of the form, please?

55.3 2 she would often fall asleep when she was reading, too. 3 he would always be ready to help other people, too. 4 she would never lock the door when she left the house 5 he would buy a newspaper every day, too. 6 they would sometimes cook a meal for the whole family, too.

55.4 1 B please 2 A Will you have B thank you. 3 A would B please.
4 A will B please?

56.1 2 She would like to go skiing on Saturday. 3 They would like roast chicken for lunch. 4 We would like to play tennis tomorrow. 5 I would like to visit Spain next summer. 6 He would like some ham sandwiches.

56.2 2 would, like to meet 3 would, like to stay 4 would, like to know 5 would, like to buy 6 would, like to pay

56.3 2 She'd like mum to make her pancakes with her tea. 3 I'd like someone to lend me an umbrella. 4 Jane would like her friends to organise a beach party. 5 They'd like their parents to book them a holiday in Greece. 6 We'd like the university to give us a grant to study abroad.

56.4 2 He would prefer to stay at home on Saturday. 3 Erin would rather eat fish than meat. 4 My brother would prefer to go to France for his holidays. 5 Alan would rather not play rugby tomorrow. 6 Denise would prefer to wear her red dress to the party.

R14.1 2 What shall I wear to the fancy dress party? 3 Shall I help you with the preparations? 4 Shall I turn right at the traffic lights? 5 Shall I go to the supermarket for you, Mum? 6 Where shall I hang my coat?

R14.2 2 We should switch off the lights when we leave an empty room. 3 We shouldn't leave the tap running when we clean our teeth. 4 We should put old bottles in the bottle bank for recycling. 5 We shouldn't cut down trees in the rainforests of the world. 6 We should protect the natural environment.

R14.3 2 a 3 d 4 b 5 f 6 e

15

Student's Book Answer Key

R14.4 2 It's pouring with rain. We had better take our umbrellas. 3 The sun is very strong now. You ought to sunbathe in the morning but not in the middle of the day. 4 It's cold in the evenings. I'd better not forget my pullover. 5 The pavement is very icy. The children ought not to run to school.

R14.5 2 Will you go shopping with me, please? 3 Would you tell me how to get to the station, please? 4 Would you close the window, please? 5 Will you drive me to the school dance, please, Dad? 6 Would you explain how to solve this problem, please?

R14.6 2 like go: She would like to go to Moscow next year. 3 They better: They had better go there by bus. It's the easiest way. 4 I like: 'What would you like to drink?' 'I'd like a cup of coffee.' 5 didn't would: He wouldn't come to the party with me. 6 bound do: They're bound to do well – they're very good students.

R14.7 2 would rather 3 Shall 4 is bound 5 would 6 should 7 are bound

F.1 2 D 3 C 4 A 5 D 6 B 7 C 8 A 9 D 10 B 11 C 12 A

F.2 2 have 3 I will go 4 better not 5 due 6 make

F.3 Student's own answers.

F.4 2 had 3 wanted 4 rather 5 should 6 going/bound 7 to 8 have/ need 9 ought 10 would

F.5 2 defendant 3 lawyers 4 punishment 5 guilty

F.6 2 had better 3 would rather not go 4 has got to 5 might visit 6 is bound to

57.1 2 d 3 a 4 f 5 b 6 e

57.2 2 Parmesan cheese is made near Parma. 3 Lots of books are borrowed from the library every day. 4 The books are printed in Hong Kong. 5 Artificial colouring isn't used in these sweets. 6 This poem was written two thousand years ago. 7 English and German are spoken here. 8 MINI cars are built in Oxford.

57.3 2 What is made in this part of the factory? 3 What are these computers used for? 4 What time are the papers usually delivered? 5 What fruit was that cake made from? 6 Who was this novel written by? 7 Which countries are giraffes found in? 8 Where were grapes first used to make wine? 9 When was rugby played for the first time? 10 Who was the Mona Lisa painted by?

58.1 2 Steel isn't produced here any more. 3 The rubbish is being cleared at the moment. 4 Our lunch is being cooked now. 5 Wooden ships were built here in the past. 6 The printing press wasn't used until the 15th century. 7 The patients were being seen when we arrived. 8 The match wasn't being played when I got there.

58.2 2 Was *Guernica* painted by Picasso? 3 Are books for adults also written by J K Rowling? 4 Is Vivaldi's *Four Seasons* being played by the orchestra? 5 What was painted on the walls by the cavemen? 6 When are the results being given out by the judges?

58.3 2 were, published 3 were, recognised 4 was played 5 is used 6 are sold

58.4 3 The bread is being baked now. 4 ✔ 5 ✔ 6 The motor car wasn't widely used before 1950.

59.1 2 had been 3 were 4 has been 5 hasn't been 6 had just been

59.2 2 e 3 a 4 c 5 f 6 d

59.3 2 Is she going to be made their next leader? 3 When will the next set of stamps be issued? 4 Will the rehearsal have been finished by midnight? 5 Where will the next Olympics be held? 6 Will the new school building have been started by the time you go there?

59.4 2 Jane's play is going to be staged at Christmas. 3 Susan's poems are going to be entered in a poetry competition. 4 Dave's short story is going to be included in an anthology. 5 Our production of *Macbeth* is going to be performed at the Summer Festival. 6 His next novel is going to be illustrated by Quentin Blake.

60.1 2 The work ought to be started before the weekend. 3 The boys ought to have been told about the trip. 4 The cooker needs to be repaired quickly. 5 Those boxes ought not to have been put there.

60.2 2 Our new television can't be mended at home. 3 Their car couldn't be used last week – it was at the garage. 4 This furniture must have been made in India. 5 The treasure might have been found by now. 6 The arrangements would have been finalised if they had had time.

60.3 2 Could the classroom be opened earlier in the morning? 3 Could they be helped by anyone? 4 Must the onions be added after the tomatoes? 5 Should the dogs be fed twice a day? 6 Ought the door to be left open during the day?

60.4 2 can be 3 must have been 4 should be 5 ought to have been 6 might have been

61.1 2 They were lent his new tent. 3 He was shown the complete range. 4 She was taught how to swim. 5 We were asked to get some butter for her. 6 I was granted permission to go there.

61.2 3 ✔ 4 We were brought some nice cakes. 5 He was offered a high salary. 6 ✔ 7 She was shown a pretty ring.

61.3 2 The book is said to be very valuable. 3 She is believed to be a beautiful girl. 4 The painting is considered to be important. 5 He is known to be a brilliant author. 6 She is supposed to be very intelligent.

62.1 2 The teacher always makes me stay late at school. 3 The doctor made Sarah go to see a specialist yesterday. 4 Working in the garden usually makes me feel very tired. 5 The film we watched last night made Jan feel very frightened. 6 Those big boys often made Paul cry when he was younger.

62.2 2 The teacher allowed Jane to stay in the classroom. 3 Tim was made to sleep on the sofa. 4 The police allowed him to go home after two hours. 5 Wendy let me wash and cut her hair. 6 The doctor allowed James to get out of bed yesterday.

62.3 2 e 3 b 4 f 5 c 6 d

62.4 2 My brother needs to have his hair cut. 3 Lucy must get her bicycle mended. 4 My mum wants to have the kitchen extended. 5 We must get the TV licence renewed.

63.1 2 taste 3 listen to 4 see 5 smell 6 feel

63.2 2 Paula heard them working in the street. 3 I noticed two students leaving school early. 4 I smelt the cabbage cooking. 5 I heard Danny coming home very late last night. 6 Jane saw him digging in the garden.

63.3 3 I've never seen an animal being hunted like that. 4 I saw him being shouted at by the teacher. 5 ✔ 6 I listened to the team coach being interviewed on TV. 7 Did you see her being awarded the prize?

63.4 2 kicking 3 burning 4 riding 5 being 6 being

R15.1 2 Was the factory started two hundred years ago? 3 Were coal and iron found in the hills? 4 Are the buses still made with iron from the hills? 5 Has production been improved in recent years? 6 Will lorries be produced here in the future?

R15.2 2 No, the fridge wasn't being repaired yesterday. 3 No, the party isn't going to be held here tomorrow. 4 No, work hadn't been started on the flat when she left. 5 No, dinner won't have been served by the time we arrive. 6 No, no changes have been made to the system yet. 7 No, your computer hasn't been repaired yet. 6 No, they won't have reached an agreement by tomorrow.

R15.3 2 When was the Sistine Chapel painted by Michelangelo? 3 When will the Italian League next be won by Napoli? 4 The Valley of the Kings in Egypt was discovered by Carter. 5 Fresh bread is baked by our baker every morning. 6 The prizes are going to be presented by Prince Charles. 7 The screenplay for the latest Thor movie was written by Chris Thornton. 8 The winning goal in the World Cup was scored by Ronaldo.

R15.4 2 d 3 f 4 b 5 a 6 e

R15.5 2 It was believed that the vases were very valuable. 3 The children were read a beautiful poem. 4 The tribes were known to be very violent. 5 Her dog is said to be a very rare breed. 6 My aunt was shown some very expensive hats.

R15.6 2 makes 3 gets/got 4 allowed 5 caused 6 needs 7 were seen 8 was heard

G.1 2 B 3 C 4 B 5 D 6 A 7 B 8 C 9 C 10 A 11 B 12 C

G.2 2 have been earned 3 has been started 4 cannot be used 5 to have died 6 had their flat

G.3 Possible answer: Strawfield Football Club was founded in 1910. Work was started on the first stadium in 1915. The club was managed by Bill Smith from 1910 to 1920. In 1952 a new stadium was built and promotion to League One was won by the team. The club was bought by Jack Lyons in 1990. The third stadium was finished in 2004.

G.4 2 be 3 haven't 4 by 5 hasn't 6 is 7 be 8 have/get 9 be 10 is

G.5 2 customers 3 childhood 4 inventions 5 old-fashioned 6 management/managers

G.6 2 are these vegetables used 3 might have been recorded 4 going to have 5 those boys break/breaking 6 her playing

Student's Book Answer Key

64.1   2 a   3 a   4 a   5 an   6 a   7 a   8 an   9 a   10 an   11 an   12 a

64.2   2 I have an uncle and a cousin in Canada.   3 A tiger is a sort of big cat.   4 A soldier always wears a uniform.   5 I got a useful present from an aunt of mine.   6 An ostrich is a large African bird.

64.3   1 an   2 An, a   3 An, a   4 A, a   5 A, an   6 An, an

64.4   3 ✔   4 ✔   5 a unique model   6 an unhappy boy   7 ✔   8 an intelligent woman

65.1   /ðə/ pear, uniform, book, one, house, pencil
/ði:/ apple, umbrella, orange, aunt, insect, angel, eggs

65.2   3 the   4 0   5 the   6 the   7 0   8 the   9 0   10 the   11 the   12 the   13 0

65.3   2 the   3 a   4 the   5 the   6 a   7 a   8 the   9 the   10 a   11 a   12 the

65.4   2 a 0, b The   3 a the, b 0   4 a The, b 0   5 a The, b 0   6 a 0, b The

66.1   3 the   4 the   5 0   6 0   7 The   8 the   9 0   10 0   11 the   12 the

66.2   2 the   3 0   4 0   5 the   6 0   7 the   8 the   9 the   10 0

66.3   2 The, the   3 the, 0   4 The, the   5 0, the   6 The, 0   7 0, the   8 the, the

66.4   2 I watched the French one.   3 I'll catch the seven o'clock one/ the one at seven o'clock.   4 I've bought the brown ones.   5 I liked the first one.   6 I'm going to visit the cheapest ones.   7 I prefer the leather one.   8 I'd like to borrow the digital one.

67.1   2 a 0, b the   3 a 0, b the   4 a the, b 0   5 a 0, b the   6 a the, b 0

67.2   3 Paper is made from wood.   4 ✔   5 ✔   6 He fought for freedom all his life.   7 ✔   8 I can't see my mother anywhere.

67.3   2 0   3 The   4 0   5 the   6 0   7 0   8 the

67.4   usually take *the*: musical instruments, categories of people, rivers, ordinal numbers, abbreviations of organisations, seas and oceans don't usually take *the*: dates and times, lakes, people's proper names, abstract nouns, materials and food, meals

R16.1   2 a   3 the   4 a   5 the   6 a   7 a   8 0   9 the   10 a   11 the   12 the   13 The   14 the   15 the   16 the   17 the   18 a   19 the   20 the   21 0   22 the   23 a   24 A   25 the   26 the   27 the   28 0   29 the   30 the

R16.2   2 an   3 a   4 an   5 an   6 an   7 a   8 a   9 an   10 an   11 an   12 a

R16.3   2 a   3 f   4 b   5 c   6 e

R16.4   with *the*: the Apennines, the Coliseum, the Archbishop, the Black Sea, the FBI, the War of Independence
without *the*: Lake Geneva, Florence, Argentina, Mount Everest, April, Liverpool Cathedral.

R16.5   2 the   3 0   4 The   5 an   6 0   7 the   8 the

R16.6   2 I went to visit the nature reserve last week.   3 She likes to go bird-watching in the spring.   4 Paul was four when he started school/Paul started school when he was four.   5 My grandparents got married after the First World War.   6 We're going to the Shetland Islands on holiday.

68.1   1 steward, stewardess   2 heir, heiress   3 actor, actress   4 duke, duchess   5 spokesman, spokeswoman   6 uncle, aunt   7 groom, bride   8 widower, widow

68.2   -s: tickets, concerts, pounds, adverts, cinemas
-es: actresses, beaches, bushes, churches, faxes
-ies: countries, ferries, parties, ladies, fairies

68.3   2 tomatoes   3 echoes   4 heroes   5 photos   6 zoos   7 Eskimos   8 logos   9 volcanoes   10 potatoes

68.4   /s/: books, students, shops, poets
/z/: theatres, pianos, paintings, novels
/ɪz/: wishes, performances, dances, stages

69.1   2 leaves   3 knives   4 lives   5 loaves   6 shelves   7 halves   8 thieves

69.2   2 feet   3 child   4 teeth   5 mouse   6 women   7 geese   8 person

69.3   2 S   3 S   4 S   5 S   6 S, P

69.4   -a: bacteria, criteria -i: stimuli, fungi -es/-s: geniuses, funguses, formulas
-es: analyses, crises -ae: formulae, antennae

69.5 2 oxen 3 children 4 women 5 men 6 loaves of bread 7 knives 8 geese
70.1 2 wood 3 Gold 4 biology 5 a good education 6 gymnastics
70.2 countable: car, vegetable, cinema, gallery, sandwich, actor, magazine
uncountable: oil, economics, sugar, health, water, poetry, sociology, ballet
70.3 2 some 3 0 4 any 5 your 6 a little 7 much
70.4 2 paper 3 a slice of 4 beer 5 a drop of 6 a jar of 7 bread 8 a bottle of 9 chocolate 10 a box of
71.1 2 hair 3 coffee 4 wines 5 homework 6 papers
71.2 2 a good time 3 bad luck 4 a noise 5 time 6 good news
71.3 2 much 3 much/any 4 many 5 some 6 much
71.4 2 a business, b businesses 3 a damages, b damage 4 a fish, b fishes/fish 5 a coffees, b coffee 6 a glass, b glasses
72.1 2 don't 3 were hidden 4 it's 5 are 6 like
72.2 2 wolves 3 a swarm of 4 ships 5 cows 6 a flock of
72.3 2 outskirts 3 barracks 4 Congratulations 5 savings 6 binoculars.
72.4 2 0 3 0 4 the 5 the, 0 6 0, 0
73.1 2 the boy's guitar 3 Paul's twin brother 4 the women's dresses 5 the animals' cages
6 your father's computer
73.2 2 Cathedral 3 surgery 4 Hospital 5 shop 6 restaurant
73.3 2 B 3 A 4 C 5 B 6 B
73.4 3 some of my cousin's books 4 ✔ 5 a team-mate of my sister's 6 one of my teacher's ideas 7 ✔
8 yesterday's newspaper
73.5 2 a bottle of my father's wine/one of my father's bottles of wine 3 two CDs of my sister's
4 this week's issue 5 today's newspaper 6 on a three-week holiday/ on three weeks' holiday
R17.1 2 princesses 3 policewoman 4 nephew 5 daughter 6 stewards 7 grandson
R17.2 2 Cities 3 discos 4 lives 5 kisses 6 parties
R17.3 2 pence 3 lice 4 sheep 5 media 6 sisters-in-law 7 pyjamas
R17.4 1 sugar 2 information 3 History 4 wine 5 petrol 6 wood 7 uncountable
R17.5 2 ✔ 3 a litre of milk 4 ✔ 5 ✔ 6 ✔ 7 a glass of wine 8 ✔ 9 a packet/bag of flour 10 ✔
R17.6 2 They went to Michael's house after the match. 3 He is a good friend of the president's.
4 We stayed at the Johnsons' villa all summer. 5 The youth hostel is open all year round.
6 Please can you get two loaves of bread from the baker's?
R17.7 2 one Picasso paintings: We saw one of Picasso's paintings at the exhibition yesterday. 3 ✔
4 Beppe restaurant: Lillian and I had dinner at Beppe's restaurant last night. 5 ✔ 6 Doris's and Liam's
house: Doris and Liam's house is opposite the playground.
R17.8 2 weeks' 3 today's 4 cousin's 5 Blair's Katie and Emma's
7 Obama's 8 dad's 9 students' 10 Tom's
H.1 2 B 3 A 4 D 5 C 6 A 7 B 8 A 9 C 10 D 11 B
H.2 2 a little 3 information 4 cups of tea 5 a lot of 6 my father's colleagues
H.3 Student's own answers.
H.4 2 ingredients 3 some 4 any 5 box 6 jar 7 little 8 butcher's 9 teas 10 tube
H.5 2 waitress 3 policemen 4 takings 5 Italian 6 professional
H.6 2 a three-week 3 some of my brother's 4 of Keats' poems 5 There was a herd
74.1 2 Mike is a good guitarist. 3 Are the band tired? 4 Has she got a nice voice? 5 The instruments are very loud. 6 It is an interesting CD. 7 Isn't Bach's music beautiful? 8 How old is that violin?
74.2 2 fast and loud. 3 beautiful old 4 high clear 5 new and fresh 6 fast, accurate and exciting 7 interesting
8 silver

Student's Book Answer Key

74.3 1 big oval yellow plastic 2 wonderful black striped silk 3 interesting long red Indian 4 simple new white cotton 5 valuable old African ebony 6 handsome tall young Asian 7 An enormous ugly 19th century red brick house. 8 A tall rectangular pink glass vase.

74.4 2 The disco was too hot. 3 The music was a little loud. 4 The concert was quite boring. 5 He wasn't good enough to be in our band. 6 It was a rather embarrassing situation. 7 The lecture wasn't very interesting. 8 The water isn't hot enough to have a bath.

75.1 2 satisfied 3 relaxed 4 embarrassing 5 shocking 6 excited

75.2 2 annoyed 3 interested 4 entertaining 5 confusing 6 excited

75.3 2 science-fiction films 3 tennis shoes 4 the school team 5 a summer holiday 6 a CD shelf 7 a music magazine 8 the living-room carpet 9 a car-washing machine 10 a vegetable garden 11 garden vegetables 12 a wine glass

75.4 2 long-bearded 3 long-haired 4 short-tailed 5 cross-eyed 6 white-backed

76.1 +er: smaller, older, cleverer
+ier: luckier, uglier, happier, earlier
more: more careful, more expensive, more extraordinary, more typical, more clever

76.2 2 Peaches are sweeter than apples. 3 John is cleverer than Paul. 4 A gold ring is more expensive than a silver ring. 5 Jane is younger than Stephanie. 6 Soccer is more popular than hockey.

76.3 2 shorter than 3 quieter 4 safer than 5 more expensive 6 more comfortable than 7 more careful

76.4 2 The Thames is longer than the Avon./The Avon is shorter than the Thames. 3 The Matterhorn is lower than Mont Blanc./Mont Blanc is higher than the Matterhorn. 4 Madonna is older than Shakira./Shakira is younger than Madonna. 5 My suitcase is lighter than Jamie's (suitcase)./Jamie's suitcase is heavier than my suitcase. 6 Everyday jeans are cheaper than brand name jeans./Brand name jeans are more expensive than everyday jeans. 7 New York was colder than Naples yesterday./Naples was warmer than New York yesterday.

77.1 2 just as bad as 3 as cheap as 4 about as tall as 5 just as pretty as 6 about as good as

77.2 2 Your guitar playing isn't as intricate as Paul's. 3 The weather today isn't as sunny as yesterday's. 4 Pauline isn't as intelligent as Julie. 5 Spielberg's films aren't as influential as Scorsese's. 6 Rhinos aren't as dangerous as elephants.

77.3 2 d 3 g 4 c 5 b 6 a 7 f

77.4 2 The watch is as expensive as the ring. 3 The sweater is as big as the cardigan. 4 The Boeing 747 is as fast as the Airbus A380. 5 The dictionary is as long as the novel. 6 Robert is as old as Samira.

78.1 2 the narrowest 3 the nicest 4 the easiest 5 the most exciting 6 the hardest 7 the heaviest 8 the palest 9 the darkest 10 the most comfortable

78.2 2 It's the funniest play I've ever seen. 3 They're the loudest band we've heard. 4 It's the prettiest village he's visited. 5 That was/is the most amazing concert I've attended. 6 It's the most dangerous place I've been to.

78.3 2 What is the highest mountain in Italy? 3 Where is the biggest city in the world? 4 How tall is the tallest man? 5 Which Italian supercar is the fastest? 6 Which is the most valuable diamond in the world?

78.4 2 the least useful invention 3 the least helpful guide 4 the least exciting match 5 the least amusing comedian 6 the least patronising person

78.5 2 the most exciting 3 the most annoying 4 the shyest 5 the least likely

79.1 2 (works) harder than 3 (drove) more carefully than 4 (arrived) later 5 (went) higher than 6 (spoke) lower than 7 (Eat) more slowly

79.2 2 more expensively 3 more loudly 4 later 5 more happily 6 more sweetly 7 more convincingly

79.3 2 as quickly as 3 as clearly as 4 just as nicely as 5 as carefully as 6 as deeply as 7 as hard as

79.4 2 Hamilton drove the fastest in the last race. 3 The children behaved most sensibly during the school trip. 4 Try to be here by 9 o'clock at the latest. 5 He helped his sick mother most thoughtfully. 6 They worked at their Italian lessons most diligently. 7 They gave to the church most generously.

80.1 2 worse 3 more 4 further 5 less 6 older/elder

80.2 2 eldest 3 worst 4 further 5 least 6 more, better

80.3 2 the farthest/furthest 3 oldest/eldest 4 the worst 5 the most 6 the least

80.4 2 John's schoolwork is getting better and better every week. 3 That was the least I could do. 4 I have just been listening to Eric Clapton's latest CD. 5 More and more people prefer sending e-mails to letters. 6 Stonehenge is one of the oldest constructions in Europe.

80.5 best latest older younger later longer most awesome

81.1 2 C 3 A 4 C 5 B 6 C 7 B 8 A

81.2 2 more than 3 more than 4 harder than 5 more (often) than 6 more than

81.3 2 e 3 d 4 b 5 f 6 a

R18.1 adjectives: 2 beautiful 3 angry 4 French, comfortable 5 new, friendly 6 dangerous
adverbs: 1 very, very well 2 beautifully 3 angrily, very 4 very 5 quite 6 very carefully 7 very late 8 fast, early

R18.2 2 interesting, interested 3 frightening, frightened 4 shocking, shocked 5 surprising, surprised 6 exhausting, exhausted

R18.3 2 a 3 f 4 b 5 c 6 g 7 h 8 e

R18.4 a Bruce b Jason c Terry d Claire
2 the thinnest 3 stronger 4 fitter 5 shorter 6 broader 7 the shortest 8 the prettiest 9 taller 10 as pretty 11 longer 12 the friendliest/most friendly 13 the most helpful

R18.5 2 bigger, biggest 3 happy, happiest 4 more exciting, most exciting 5 shallower, shallowest 6 good, better 7 heavy, heaviest 8 more patient, most patient 9 farther/further, farthest/furthest 10 white, whiter

R18.6 2 easier than 3 more tiring than 4 more exotic, than 5 more handsome than 6 worse than

R18.7 2 more slowly 3 better 4 harder 5 more loudly 6 more carefully

R18.8 the sweetest nicer the strangest wider cleaner as big smaller cosier

I.1 2 B 3 C 4 A 5 D 6 B 7 C 8 A 9 C 10 B 11 D 12 A

I.2 2 shorter than 3 more slowly than 4 as hard as 5 more money than

I.3 Student's own answer.

I.4 2 very 3 most 4 as 5 different 6 the 7 least 8 of 9 enough

I.5 2 deafening 3 dangerous 4 easily 5 enjoyable

I.6 2 my last day 3 the most beautifully (of all) 4 many nice birthday 5 the slowest (walker) 6 a large bright

82.1 2 He 3 it 4 I 5 They 6 she 7 We

82.2 2 c 3 f 4 e 5 d 6 a

82.3 2 It/She 3 You 4 It 5 It 6 you 7 It, it

82.4 2 it 3 me 4 us 5 her 6 them 7 you

82.5 2 I 3 you 4 you 5 them 6 him 7 They 8 me 9 you 10 I

83.1 2 her 3 its 4 your 5 Their 6 his (own)

83.2 2 His 3 their 4 her 5 It's 6 they're

83.3 2 hers 3 mine 4 his 5 ours 6 theirs

83.4 2 Their 3 his 4 His 5 Her 6 their 7 their 8 their 9 Their 10 Hers

84.1 2 a 3 b 4 f 5 c 6 e

84.2 2 You will amuse yourselves this afternoon. 3 We washed ourselves in the river when we were camping. 4 He walked to the table and helped himself to the food. 5 Nobody understands how Sandra hurt herself. 6 I can't stand people who always talk about themselves.

84.3 1 He likes to spend time by himself. 2 She was by herself all week. 3 They did it by themselves. 4 You can work by yourself today. 5 We travelled around Spain by ourselves. 6 I have made a wonderful cake by myself. 7 You can't leave a baby by itself in the house. 8 He was able to run the firm by himself.

85.1 2 These are foreign visitors. 3 Those are photos of our capital cities. 4 Are these your maps? 5 Where are these families from? 6 What are those flags?

Student's Book Answer Key

85.2 2 Take these three glasses, please. 3 Bring me those two vases, please. 4 Close that small box, please. 5 Take this new umbrella, please. 6 Give me those photographs, please.

85.3 2 that 3 This 4 this 5 that 6 that

85.4 2 those 3 Those 4 these 5 These 6 Those

86.1 2 e 3 b 4 f 5 d 6 a

86.2 Possible answers: 2 I usually read a weekly one. 3 I wear Italian ones. 4 I support a British one. 5 I like small and sweet ones. 6 I choose relaxing ones.

86.3 2 a new one 3 a French one 4 Which one 5 another one 6 a blue one

86.4 2 one 3 Which one 4 The ones 5 one 6 ones

87.1 2 All 3 everything 4 All 5 Everything 6 everyone

87.2 2 Each of 3 each other 4 applicant 5 every 6 one another

87.3 2 Every 3 All 4 Everything 5 Every 6 everything 7 Everybody

87.4 2 each other/one another 3 each/all 4 everything 5 Everyone/Everybody 6 everywhere

88.1 2 either 3 Neither 4 both 5 Neither 6 either

88.2 2 can take neither of them 3 can't remember either of them 4 can go to neither 5 don't want to watch either

88.3 2 neither of 3 both 4 Neither of 5 both 6 either of 7 Both

88.4 2 Neither, nor 3 neither, nor 4 either, or 5 both, and 6 neither, nor 7 either, or

89.1 1 any, some 2 any 3 any, any 4 some 5 any, some 6 any 7 any, some

89.2 2 Did you spend any money yesterday? 3 He hasn't done/He isn't doing any work this morning. 4 There aren't/weren't any apples in the shop. 5 Did she find any new clothes last Saturday? 6 They didn't like any of the flats they saw last week.

89.3 2 are no 3 aren't any 4 Are, no 5 were none 6 Have, had none

89.4 2 f 3 d 4 a 5 c 6 e

90.1 2 many 3 much 4 much 5 many 6 much 7 much 8 much

90.2 2 enough 3 all 4 too many 5 most 6 too much

90.3 2 There aren't enough sandwiches for everybody to have one. 3 Are there enough people here for us to start? 4 Do you think this box is big enough? 5 We've seen enough of this film, thank you. 6 He isn't clever enough to pass the exam. 7 Have you had enough to eat? 8 Did they have enough room in the car for the dog?

90.4 2 many 3 Most 4 all 5 lot 6 all

91.1 2 somebody 3 somewhere 4 something 5 somewhere 6 Something

91.2 2 Did you see anybody you knew at the conference? 3 Have you given him anything for his birthday? 4 Have you seen my office keys anywhere? 5 Is there anything I could bring you from Japan? 6 Did anybody take my scarf home by mistake last Friday?

91.3 2 is nothing 3 isn't anywhere 4 didn't tell me anything 5 went nowhere 6 isn't anyone

91.4 2 a 3 b 4 f 5 d 6 c

92.1 2 Nobody sings as well as Patsy. 3 Nowhere in the world is like Venice. 4 Nothing is as interesting as Nature. 5 Nowhere is as exciting as London. 6 Nothing is as important to me as my wedding ring.

92.2 2 d 3 a 4 c 5 b 6 e

92.3 3 ✔ 4 Nobody famous came to the opening. 5 No one turned up on time. 6 ✔ 7 ✔ 8 Nothing unusual was seen there.

92.4 2 however 3 whenever 4 wherever 5 whatever 6 Whoever 7 Whoever 8 whatever

R19.1 2 his 3 their 4 him 5 him 6 his 7 their 8 your 9 you 10 their 11 they 12 us/me 13 his 14 they

R19.2 2 theirs 3 hers 4 yours 5 mine 6 ours

R19.3 2 enjoyed ourselves 3 washed itself 4 bought myself 5 Ask yourself 6 found themselves

R19.4	2 that 3 Those 4 this 5 Those 6 This
R19.5	2 Everyone 3 either 4 Nobody 5 whatever 6 hot enough 7 Neither 8 else
R19.6	2 e 3 b 4 f 5 d 6 c
R19.7	2 anything 3 nothing 4 Everything 5 something 6 anything
R19.8	2 D 3 D 4 C 5 C 6 B 7 D 8 C
J.1	2 B 3 D 4 A 5 C 6 B 7 D 8 A 9 C 10 B 11 C 12 D
J.2	2 isn't anyone 3 knows everything 4 everything 5 No one / Nobody knows 6 nowhere
J.3	Student's own answer.
J.4	2 whenever 3 either 4 nothing 5 something 6 both 7 anything 8 somewhere 9 Someone/Somebody 10 no one/nobody
J.5	2 personnel 3 appointments 4 advertisement 5 employee/employees 6 consideration
J.6	2 haven't got any suitable 3 mind either English Cheddar (cheese) 4 a lot of 5 that whole box of 6 wasn't enough room
93.1	2 twelve 3 hundred 4 eight 5 twenty 6 thirty-three 7 two 8 seventeen one, two, eight, twelve, seventeen, twenty, thirty-three, hundred
93.2	2 one thousand kilometres 3 fifty-two pounds 4 thirty-nine point five degrees Celsius 5 seventy-eight per cent 6 telephone: five-five/double five-nine-eight-oh-two-six 7 one thousand three hundred and seventy-six euros 8 ten thousand six hundred and forty dollars
93.3	2 love 3 nil 4 oh 5 nought/zero 6 nought/zero 7 oh 8 nought/zero
93.4	2 several hundred 3 Forty-four 4 thousand 5 out of 6 Millions 7 cent 8 four thousand five hundred
93.5	2 d 3 e 4 f 5 c 6 a
94.1	2 second 3 third 4 fourth 5 fifth 6 sixth 7 seventh 8 eighth 9 ninth 10 tenth 11 eleventh 12 twelfth
94.2	2 the twenty-first 3 thirteenth 4 Twentieth 5 millionth 6 a hundredth 7 the forty-fourth
94.3	2 24.03.08/03.24.08 3 55 B.C. 4 18.12.1834/12.18.1834 5 1908 6 2001 7 33 B.C.
94.4	2 2/9 3 4/7 4 ½ 5 5/8 6 3/100 7 7/15 8 3/5 9 2/3
95.1	2 which 3 who 4 who 5 which 6 who
95.2	2 I was working with 3 we were talking about 4 you are waiting for 5 he rowed across the Atlantic in 6 he went to the party with 7 he lived in as a boy
95.3	2 She is the girl whose mother is a famous painter. 3 We are the students whose bags were stolen. 4 I am the man whose music was played at the wedding. 5 They are the people whose house caught fire. 6 You are the one whose essay was brilliant.
95.4	3 ✔ 4 ✔ 6 ✔
95.5	2 The dog that was found in the park is Mr Ross's. 3 This is the girl I gave the flowers to. 4 The phone call I was waiting for arrived too late. 5 This is the new car I'm going to buy. 6 That's the teacher who gives us lots of homework.
96.1	2 ND 3 ND 4 D 5 ND 6 D
96.2	2 who/whom 3 which 4 whose 5 which 6 who
96.3	2 who 3 who/whom 4 who/whom 5 who 6 who
96.4	2 Mrs Sarandon, whose daughter was in the same class as my sister, returned from the USA two weeks ago. 3 My boss, who I've worked for for twenty years/for whom I've worked for twenty years, is going to retire next December. 4 Malindi, which is a popular holiday resort, is in Kenya. 5 Nicole Kidman, who has made a lot of Hollywood movies, was born in Australia. 6 The Beatles, whose name then was The Silver Beatles, first played together at the Cavern Club. 7 *Crypto*, whose author is Dan Brown, is a novel based on the world of computers. 8 The Eiffel Tower, which was built between 1887 and 1889, is the most famous landmark in Paris. 9 The Olympic Games, which were held at Olympia in ancient times, were first revived in Athens in 1896. 10 The Smiths, who have just sold their house in the UK, are buying a house in Chicago.
97.1	2 where 3 when 4 when 5 where 6 when
97.2	2 that 3 that 4 – 5 – 6 that

Student's Book Answer Key

97.3 2 e 3 b 4 f 5 d 6 a

97.4 2 which was illustrated 3 who were playing 4 which was eating 5 who was taking 6 which was covering 7 which was painted 8 who are digging

R20.1 2 a 3 g 4 c 5 h 6 b 7 f 8 e

R20.2 2 three hundred and fifty-seven 3 seventeen point four 4 eight thousand nine hundred and twenty-six 5 nought point three four 6 four hundred and twenty-five thousand 7 fifty thousand 8 ten thousand eight hundred and seventy-three

R20.3 2 which 3 (who)/(whom) 4 whose 5 what 6 whose 7 which 8 (which)/(that)

R20.4 2 minus eighty-nine point two degrees Celsius/centigrade 3 five thousand 4 nine million 5 one million seven hundred thousand dollars 6 four hundred and seventy dollars 7 two-thirds 8 fifty seven point eight degrees Celsius/centigrade

R20.5 2 The old oak tree which was in our garden fell down last night. 3 The footballers, who all played well, celebrated after the game. 4 My friend, whose sister is a dancer, gave me a CD. 5 Captain Caldwell, who/whom I met last summer, sailed to Australia. 6 Arthur, who is very good at chess, lives next door. 7 My car, which is getting rather old, is painted green. 8 Your sister, who is tall for her age, is very pretty.

R20.6 2 ✔ 5 ✔ 6 ✔ 8 ✔

R20.7 2 in whom 3 for whom 4 with whom 5 about whom 6 without whom 7 under whom 8 to whom

98.1 2 Whose MP3 player is it? 3 Who were you talking to on Skype? 4 Who did you write about on Wikipedia? 5 Whose laptop did you use? 6 Whose lecture did you hear? 7 Whose mobile is that? 8 Who were you chatting with last night?

98.2 2 What 3 What 4 Which 5 Which 6 What 7 What 8 Which

98.3 2 Whose CDs are these? 3 What is that computer? 4 Which is his memory stick? 5 Whose is this SatNav? 6 Which cables are ours? 7 Whose laptop is this? 8 Which are your earphones? 9 What time is it? 10 Which suitcase is mine?

98.4 2 What long legs that man has got! 3 What sweet puppies they are! 4 What a wonderful cook she is! 5 What an excellent teacher Mr Smith is! 6 What a comfortable hotel it is! 7 What a small mobile phone this is! 8 What brilliant video games those are!

99.1 2 Where 3 When 4 How 5 Where 6 Why 7 When 8 How

99.2 2 much 3 many 4 much 5 much 6 many 7 many 8 much

99.3 2 big 3 old 4 often 5 wide 6 long 7 high 8 deep

99.4 2 What/How about visiting your parents tomorrow? 3 What/How about watching a DVD tonight? 4 What/How about cooking spaghetti for dinner? 5 What/How about playing a computer game later? 6 What/How about taking the dog for a walk? 7 What/How about sending an email to our German friends? 8 What/How about downloading some music on our iPod?

100.1 2 'Are the boys playing football now?' 'Yes, they are.' 3 'Did she feed the dogs this morning?' 'No, she didn't.' 4 'Have you ever been to Venice?' 'No, I haven't.' 5 'Can she swim very strongly?' 'Yes, she can.' 6 'Is your mother cooking lunch tomorrow?' 'No, she isn't.'

100.2 2 When can you download those pictures for me? 3 How long does it take to install this program? 4 Where is the decoder for the satellite channels? 5 Why are you still using that dial-up connection? 6 Who knows how to operate this new Microsoft system?

100.3 2 Wasn't she on the trip yesterday? 3 Wouldn't you like to come with us? 4 Can't you ask him to help them? 5 Won't she play her guitar for me? 6 Didn't he travel there by train last week?

100.4 2 g 3 c 4 b 5 a 6 h 7 e 8 f
Subject: 2 Who 3 Which 4 Who 5 What 7 Which 8 What
Complement: 1 Who 6 Which

101.1 2 wasn't it? 3 haven't you? 4 won't he? 5 wouldn't they? 6 hadn't she? 7 didn't she? 8 didn't he? 9 weren't they? 10 hasn't she?

101.2 2 d 3 b 4 f 5 a 6 h 7 e 8 g

101.3 2 wasn't 3 had 4 have 5 would 6 didn't 7 isn't 8 have

101.4 2 Is it really? 3 Was he really? 4 Didn't they really? 5 Don't you really? 6 Wouldn't they really? 7 Didn't you really? 8 Does she really?

102.1 2 So does he. 3 So did they. 4 So is she. 5 So would I. 6 So will we. 7 So does she. 8 So have I.

102.2 2 B 3 C 4 B 5 A 6 C

102.3 2 d 3 a 4 f 5 c 6 e

102.4 2 hope so 3 don't think so 4 expect so 5 suppose not 6 am afraid so 7 guess so 8 am afraid not

R21.1 2 about 3 with 4 like 5 to 6 from 7 to 8 after

R21.2 2 Who 3 Which 4 What 5 Why 6 Whose 7 Where 8 When

R21.3 2 many 3 often 4 large 5 long 6 much 7 about 8 big

R21.4 2 c 3 a 4 b 5 f 6 e

R21.5 2 Does she play handball every week? Yes, she does. 3 Is he the boy you like? No, he isn't. 4 Did they visit the Forum last week? Yes, they did. 5 Have you ever been to Africa? No, I haven't. 6 Are you going to the cinema tomorrow? Yes, I am. 7 Can he sit next to you? No, he can't. 8 Would you like another cup of coffee? No, I wouldn't.

R21.6 2 do they 3 is he 4 didn't we 5 would she 6 can't they 7 had you 8 hasn't she

R21.7 2 So 3 Neither/Nor 4 did 5 not 6 not 7 would 8 so

K.1 2 C 3 C 4 D 5 D 6 C 7 D 8 A 9 C 10 D 11 C 12 A

K.2 2 three-quarters 3 about joining 4 (that/which) I rode 5 where 6 all 105

K.3 Student's own answer.

K.4 2 which 3 that 4 where 5 whose 6 who 7 which 8 which/that 9 who 10 When

K.5 2 concerned 3 Global 4 denial 5 production 6 disastrous

K.6 2 one quarter 3 the day on which 4 who were queuing 5 didn't either

103.1 2 strictly 3 easily 4 publicly 5 badly 6 correctly 7 quietly 8 happily

103.2 1 strongly, quickly, softly 2 angrily, lazily, luckily 3 possibly, comfortably, probably 4 technically, politically, anatomically

103.3 2 quickly 3 quiet 4 correctly 5 happily 6 good 7 well 8 hard 9 hardly 10 slow

103.4 2 d 3 b 4 e 5 a 6 c

103.5 2 well 3 happily 4 nearly 5 badly 6 quickly 7 hardly 8 slowly

104.1 2 next week 3 last year 4 this month 5 now 6 yesterday

104.2 2 You must go to Cannes if you haven't been yet. 3 I have just met your lovely wife. 4 Unfortunately the tickets have already been sold. 5 Have you heard any good gossip recently?

104.3 2 When do you usually surf the Internet? 3 Do you always play tennis when the weather is fine? 4 Does he ever play the piano any more? 5 Do you still see her occasionally/Do you occasionally still see her?

104.4 2 is still a popular film 3 was again given 4 will start shortly 5 no longer allow 6 rarely go to bed

105.1 2 not very 3 rather 4 fairly 5 extremely 6 too

105.2 2 disgusting 3 wrong 4 happy 5 full 6 certain

105.3 2 He was so tired he could barely speak. 3 Your new puppy is so sweet! 4 I don't think the car is big enough for everyone. 5 Our new boss is such a nice person! 6 The state of the roads is absolutely disgraceful here.

105.4 2 too 3 well 4 quite 5 such 6 enough

105.5 2 c 3 b 4 e 5 f 6 a

106.1 2 Rome and Florence are extremely beautiful cities. 3 Cyprus seems a good place for a holiday. 4 She finished writing her essay carefully. 5 I feel very well after a week in the mountains. 6 My teacher was pleased with my progress.

106.2 2 c-b-a 3 a-c-b 4 b-a-c 5 c-b-a 6 b-a-c

106.3 2 does he get 3 have we experienced 4 had I left 5 is the story 6 have I seen

Student's Book Answer Key

106.4 2 if they play harder can they win this match 3 after I've finished cooking can I help you with your homework 4 by doing it this way will you take good photos

107.1 2 on 3 in 4 on, in 5 in 6 in 7 at, at 8 at

107.2 2 on 3 at 4 At 5 on 6 at 7 in 8 At 9 in 10 at

107.3 2 d 3 f 4 b 5 c 6 a

107.4 2 on 3 In the end 4 in 5 at the end 6 At first

107.5 1 in 2 in 3 at 4 in the morning/afternoon/evening/at night 5 in + Student's own answers.

108.1 2 between Oxford and Cambridge 3 of a number from 1 to 20 4 in the States between January and April 5 in Africa from 1995 to 2002 6 between today and Thursday

108.2 2 for 3 since 4 since 5 for 6 since 7 for 8 since

108.3 2 within 3 until 4 before 5 by 6 after

108.4 2 e 3 f 4 c 5 a 6 b

109.1 2 the, 0 3 the 4 the 5 0 6 the 7 0 8 the

109.2 2 e 3 b 4 f 5 a 6 c

109.3 2 below 3 above 4 beneath 5 over 6 underneath

109.4 2 at 3 on 4 in 5 on 6 at 7 on 8 on 9 in 10 on 11 in, at 12 in, at

110.1 2 between, and 3 behind, in front of 4 opposite 5 along 6 among

110.2 2 along 3 between 4 around 5 among 6 from

110.3 2 on the corner 3 at the corner 4 at the back 5 in the front 6 on the back

110.4 2 f 3 b 4 a 5 d 6 c

111.1 2 take 3 returned 4 was sent 5 get 6 come 7 drive

111.2 3 ✔ 4 ✔ 5 He's staying at the Astoria Hotel. 6 My father's ill in hospital. 7 Tim fell off his motorbike.

111.3 2 into 2 onto 4 onto 5 into 6 into 7 onto

111.4 2 from 3 of 4 off 5 off /onto 6 onto 7 into

112.1 2 along 3 towards 4 across 5 through 6 past

112.2 2 at 3 for 4 past 5 to 6 in

112.3 2 c 3 e 4 f 5 a 6 d

112.4 2 at 3 in 4 to 5 for 6 up to

112.5 2 at 3 along/down/up 4 as far as 5 on 6 on 7 At 8 past 9 in 10 on

113.1 2 to 3 to 4 for 5 for 6 to

113.2 2 Can you pass my wife this sandwich, please? 3 My mother made Linda a new dress. 4 Dad bought Mark a scooter. 5 Susie's eyes are bad, so will you read her this letter? 6 My sister's new boyfriend says she's going to teach him English.

113.3 2 She reported them to the police. 3 I lent her my school books. 4 He showed us his stamp collection. 5 We sang them a traditional song. 6 They bought me some nice presents for Christmas./They bought some nice Christmas presents for me.

113.4 2 I was introduced to the actor at a party. 3 The passage was dictated to the students. 4 Paul's holiday was described to me in great detail. 5 The incident was reported to her early next morning. 6 I was told the story when I went to see them.

114.1 2 by 3 on 4 on 5 in 6 by 7 on 8 in

114.2 2 of 3 without 4 with 5 by 6 with 7 of 8 by

114.3 2 a 3 b 4 f 5 d 6 c

114.4 2 without asking 3 about winning the first prize 4 for making so much noise 5 with stealing the painting 6 by falling off a ladder 7 to getting up so early

R22.1 2 tidily 3 fast 4 helpful 5 terribly 6 well 7 easy 8 badly 9 aggressively 10 hard 11 beautifully 12 lucky

R22.2 2 My mother has recently come back from the USA/has come back from the USA recently. 3 Have you finished your homework yet? 4 Paul has never been to Greece. 5 My parents hadn't been to a rock concert before. 6 I have just seen Robbie Williams in the street. 7 I'm not hungry, thanks – I've already eaten/I've eaten already. 8 I haven't been skiing lately. 9 We don't usually eat out at the weekend.

R22.3 2 d 3 f 4 a 5 c 6 e

R22.4 2 at 3 by 4 on 5 from 6 between 7 along 8 behind

R22.5 2 in 3 on 4 on 5 in 6 at 7 on 8 on 9 at 10 in

R22.6 2 since 3 for 4 for 5 since 6 for 7 for 8 since

R22.7 2 A 3 A 4 C 5 A 6 B 7 C 8 B 9 B 10 C

L.1 2 C 3 C 4 D 5 A 6 A 7 B 8 A 9 D 10 C 11 B 12 B

L.2 2 any more 3 such a 4 have I seen 5 you work hard 6 cakes to your

L.3 Student's own answer.

L.4 2 always 3 never 4 before/by 5 with 6 during 7 in 8 to 9 into 10 by

L.5 2 restoration 3 absolutely 4 laborious 5 polishing

L.6 2 were told about 3 by begging 4 Only by walking/Only if you walk 5 No sooner had he finished 6 such an easy exam

115.1 2 tells 3 said 4 says 5 tell 6 said 7 told 8 say

115.2 2 He didn't say anything to me yesterday. 3 They have just told me about the concert. 4 Don't tell anyone our plans for the trip. 5 Remember to tell her to wear comfortable shoes. 6 I wonder what she will say to us at the meeting tomorrow.

115.3 say: a word, goodbye, yes, a prayer, thank you, something wrong
tell: the time, the difference, me about..., a lie, a story, you how to...

115.4 2 told 3 said 4 said 5 tell 6 tell 7 tell 8 say 9 saying 10 tell

116.1 2 d 3 f 4 c 5 b 6 a

116.2 2 Mike warned us/me it was dangerous not to use sun cream in that heat. 3 Lucy advised Dave to leave his camera behind if he went to those streets. 4 Dick reminded the boys not to swim when the red flag was out. 5 The teacher told the class to stop making that noise. 6 Smith ordered Johnson to get out and never come back.

116.3 2 her, looks 3 are 4 couldn't 5 die 6 she wants, they 7 his, own

116.4 2 explained 3 stated 4 recommended 5 claimed 6 answered

117.1 2 they 3 he 4 they 5 I 6 he

117.2 2 the following month 3 that 4 the night before 5 the following day 6 those

117.3 2 Suzie said that she was going out on her scooter then. 3 Bill said that he had fallen off his BMX bike eight times the day before. 4 Christine said that she had really enjoyed water skiing the previous summer. 5 Dave said that he hadn't heard that CD before I played it. 6 Mark said that they were going to go paragliding the following day. 7 Johnny said that he would go and help them. 8 Louisa said that she would love to fly in a micro-light. 9 Pauline said that she would have enjoyed climbing Everest.

118.1 2 Julia asked Elena if she often went skiing. 3 Rob asked Mick if he had ever been to Siena 4 Jo asked the children if they were enjoying themselves. 5 Angela asked if Muriel ate meat. 6 George asked if Donald was happy in his new job.

118.2 2 Sammy wanted to know how they were going to travel to Spain. 3 Alex inquired where we/I would go for our/my holidays. 4 Joyce asked why I had phoned him the previous evening. 5 Brian wondered who had read that novel. 6 Laura wanted to know what the time was.

118.3 2 f 3 a 4 e 5 c 6 d

118.4 2 Liz suggested eating/that we ate at the new Turkish restaurant the following day. 3 Luke recommended that I/we toured the Greek islands the following summer. 4 June suggested organising /that we organised a party to raise money for the WWF. 5 Martha recommended that Paul stayed in and rested. 6 Lois suggested not doing/that we didn't do anything energetic the following week.

27

Student's Book Answer Key

R23.1 2 told 3 tell 4 said 5 said 6 tell 7 told 8 said

R23.2 2 'I am sending you to a specialist,' said Doctor Smith. 3 'Don't drive too fast here again,' warned the policeman. 4 'You haven't done your homework properly,' said the teacher. 5 'You are all lazy,' the manager said. 6 'Remember to buy a birthday card for Anne,' said Janice.

R23.3 3 ✔ 4 Dilys told him the news. 5 ✔ 6 I told them everything I knew. 7 ✔ 8 Lucy told them the results.

R23.4 2 we 3 him 4 they 5 I 6 them

R23.5 2 Louis asked when it had happened. 3 The manager asked why I was standing there. 4 Lynn asked who they would work with the following week. 5 The doctor asked how I had managed to do that. 6 The customer asked how much oranges cost.

R23.6 2 I wanted any more tea. 3 had had some trouble with his bike. 4 she was all right. 5 I didn't open a savings account. 6 to get out of his car.

R23.7 I asked her if she was such a good swimmer and she answered that she wasn't. But she said that Sally had got a new boyfriend who was very sporty. He did paragliding, rafting and canyoning. And scuba diving. I said that then I saw why she had picked scuba diving. She probably thought it was the least dangerous of all. I asked if she had done that for long and Jane replied that Sally had done it for a about a month, that she quite liked it now and had become more confident.

119.1 2 would feel 3 would find out, would be 4 would you do 5 would be 6 Would you buy 7 wouldn't take, would get 8 wouldn't mind

119.2 2 Peter believed it would rain that afternoon. 3 Anne thought Paul wouldn't get there in time to help. 4 Dick knew his friends would be waiting for him at the airport. 5 Ellie promised to finish/she'd finish her project by the following day. 6 Bill hoped John would remember to take his guitar.

119.3 2 Could/Would 3 could/might, might/would 4 should 5 should 6 Couldn't, wouldn't

119.4 2 I wouldn't have gone by car. I would have gone by train. 3 A low-cost flight would have cost about the same as the train. 4 Would you really have spent all this money on clothes? 5 They should have been more careful. 6 He couldn't have come earlier. 7 They might not have been listening. 8 They could have played much better.

120.1 2 If you want to install sat nav in a car, you just need a bracket to fix the device to the windscreen. 3 If you have a cigarette lighter on the dashboard, you can use it as a power source. 4 If you type in the destination post code, the sat nav system gives you the best route. 5 If you install special software, you can find out the road conditions, traffic information and speed limits.

120.2 2 d 3 f 4 a 5 c 6 e

120.3 2 If you want to meet Michael, you'll have to come back tomorrow. 3 If he hopes to pass the exam, he'll need to study much harder. 4 If they work this hard, they'll finish the job very quickly. 5 If she doesn't drive more slowly, she'll have an accident. 6 If we don't use a computer, it'll take too long.

120.4 2 If he's trying pot-holing, he should go with an expert. 3 If they are thinking of going paragliding, they can buy my old equipment. 4 If you are travelling through the Amazon, you might need a guide. 5 If she's skating on the lake, she must check the ice.

121.1 2 1 3 2 4 0 5 0 6 2 7 1 8 1

121.2 2 If Lucy went to Rome, John would follow her there. 3. If the Johnsons didn't invite me to their Christmas party, I'd be happier. 4 If I knew how to play American football, I'd explain it to you. 5 If you read Harry Potter, I'm sure you'd enjoy it. 6 If we cycled to Devon, we'd feel exhausted by the end of the day. 7 If I were younger, I'd go on a backpacking tour around Europe. 8 I wouldn't be surprised if he arrived now. He's always late.

121.3 2 might 3 could 4 would like 5 should 6 were 7 shouldn't

121.4 2 found 3 would she go 4 crashed 5 left 6 invited

122.1 2 f 3 3 h 2 4 c 1 5 g 0 6 d 3 7 e 1 8 a 2

122.2 2 If she had known about the new snowfall, she wouldn't have gone snowboarding. 3 If she hadn't been on her snowboard, she wouldn't have had the accident. 4 If they hadn't enjoyed extreme sports, they would have stayed at home. 5 If Lewis Hamilton hadn't driven so well, he wouldn't have become world champion. 6 If Sally had listened to her boyfriend, she would have taken up scuba diving.

122.3 2 Would he have passed the exam? Yes, if he had worked harder.   3 Would they have enjoyed the show? Yes, if it had been shorter.   4 Would she have won the competition? Yes, if she hadn't fallen over.   5 Would you have eaten all that food? Yes, if I hadn't already had dinner.   6 Would he have worked in Argentina? Yes, if he hadn't accepted the job in Spain.

123.1 2 But for   3 in case   4 unless   5 provided that   6 When

123.2 2 They wish they could win the world cup.   3 I wish I was/could be 10 cm taller.   4 Barbara wishes John would/could come back from the USA soon.   5 We wish our neighbours wouldn't be so noisy.   6 She wishes she could act with Johnny Depp.   7 I wish I had/could have a brand new motorbike.

123.3 2 If only Mike hadn't lost his job (in a bank)!   3 I wish Sue hadn't gone on holiday without me.   4 If only Dave hadn't lost his wallet (in the market)!   5 If only John hadn't run off with my best friend!   6 I wish I had been luckier.

123.4 3 ✔ 4 Don't forget your sun lotion, just in case it gets hot.   5 The team would have lost but for Dave's brilliant goal.   6 ✔

R24.1 2 f 3 a 4 e 5 d 6 c

R24.2 2 doesn't have 3 would have 4 will lend 5 would enjoy 6 wouldn't have been

R24.3 2 What would he think if you did that?   3 What does she say if he goes out at night?   4 Where would you have gone if you had had the money?   5 How will they meet if she moves to Milan?   6 How much would you have to pay if you rented this flat?   7 Who tries hard if they don't have a good reason?   8 Why would he have invited her out if he hadn't liked her/didn't like her?

R24.4 2 had, would   3 would, had   4 would, had

R24.5 2 If he behaves like that, we'll get into trouble.   3 If he hadn't dropped the ball, he would have scored.   4 If you don't stop doing that, I will get very angry.   5 If she wants a new hairstyle, she goes to the hairdresser's.   6 If he arrived earlier, we'd leave on time.

R24.6 2 would have   3 could   4 should have   5 might have   6 may

R24.7 2 If I were her, I wouldn't work such long hours.   3 If I were them, I'd take it to the mechanic.   4 If I were you, I'd ask the bank for a loan.   5 If I were their mother, I wouldn't let them go.   6 If I were him, I'd take a break.

M.1 2 C 3 B 4 D 5 C 6 A 7 B 8 D 9 B 10 A 11 C

M.2 2 drove   3 only   4 would/could   5 he would   6 your helping me

M.3 Paul told John that he should give Mary some of the money they had found. John said he wasn't going to because she'd show it to everyone and they'd be in trouble. Paul said he was sure she wouldn't say anything to anyone.

M.4 2 won   3 put   4 wanted   5 were   6 spend   7 couldn't   8 would   9 could   10 enjoy

M.5 1 bakery   2 tantalising   3 selection   4 disappointment   5 watering   6 parking

M.6 2 asked me if I wanted   3 unless you ask   4 you should get hungry   5 warned me not to

124.1 2 She cooked on both Saturday and Sunday. 3 We drank both white and red wine.   4 He had both lunch and dinner at home.   5 She wants both a starter and a main course.   6 Both Paul and Jane have eaten enough.

124.2 2 either a Jonathan or a Cox   3 neither polite nor fast   4 neither cheap nor good 5 either a carrot or a tomato soup 6 neither long nor interesting

124.3 2 however   3 on the other hand   4 though   5 However   6 on the other hand

124.4 2 d 3 f 4 a 5 b 6 e

124.5 2 and   3 and   4 but   5 and   6 or 7 both   8 however/tough

125.1 2 because   3 Since   4 As   5 because   6 Since

125.2 2 so often that   3 so as to   4 so tasty that   5 so as not to   6 so   7 such a good

125.3 2 g 3 f 4 a 5 d 6 b 7 e

  2 He went out in the rain and as a result he caught a bad cold.   3 He forgot to feed his goldfish and consequently it died.   4 It's a very important matter and therefore I don't want any questions.   5 It's a secret and for this reason we mustn't say anything to anyone.   6 He was feeling bored so he switched on the radio.   7 He has been lifting heavy weights and as a result he's got backache.

Student's Book Answer Key

125.4 2 in order to 3 so that 4 so that 5 in order to 6 so that 7 to 8 to

126.1 2 until 3 as long as 4 while 5 Whenever 6 as soon as

126.2 2 before 3 after 4 After 5 After 6 before

126.3 2 Then 3 After that 4 Next 5 until 6 Finally

126.4 2 Wash your hands before eating dinner. 3 We ran outside as soon as the lesson was over. 4 She gets very excited whenever there's a birthday party. 5 He got a wonderful job after leaving school. 6 You'll just have to wait until I've finished.

127.1 2 A 3 C 4 A 5 B 6 C 7 A 8 C

127.2 2 She's not as fit as she used to be. 3 This book is much more interesting than I expected. 4 They played as they'd never played before. 5 Your painting is much better than mine.

127.3 2 d 3 f 4 a 5 b 6 e

127.4 2 Linda told me that she doesn't like Steve. 3 I don't think that it matters very much. 4 Pat's mother hopes that she will go to college. 5 Will you promise that you won't tell anyone? 6 Danny was sure that nobody had seen him.

128.1 2 il- 3 ir- 4 in- 5 un- 6 im-

128.2 2 undercooked 3 overheat 4 overestimated 5 underachieve 6 overcharged

128.3 2 f 3 b 4 c 5 d 6 a

128.4 2 co-exist 3 deforestation 4 misfortunes 5 remix 6 cooperate

128.5 2 de 3 bi 4 over 5 mis 6 over 7 dis 8 over

129.1 2 -ation 3 -ships 4 -hood 5 -ment 6 -ance

129.2 2 Swedish 3 Austrian 4 Portuguese 5 Bolivian 6 Polish 7 Japanese 8 Scottish 9 Irish 10 English 11 Hungarian 12 Chilean 13 Canadian 14 Danish 15 Chinese

129.3 2 -less 3 -ical 4 -ize/-ise 5 -fy 6 -en

129.4 2 careful 3 childhood, pleasant 4 romantic, sentimental 5 tiny 6 Japanese, fashionable

129.5 2 powerful 3 cordless 4 player 5 noisy 6 alcoholic 7 Thicken 8 fashionable

130.1 2 approve 3 apologise 4 applied 5 will ask 6 agree 7 was dreaming 8 thank

130.2 2 to 3 from 4 at 5 about 6 for 7 to 8 in

130.3 2 f 3 a 4 c 5 b 6 e

130.4 2 look after 3 look up 4 are looking into 5 looked at 6 looked for

130.5 2 charged 3 to pay 4 thinking 5 leave 6 apply 7 believe 8 congratulate

131.1 2 am bored 3 was ashamed 4 was born 5 is busy 6 was disappointed 7 were angry

131.2 2 d 3 f 4 c 5 b 6 a

131.3 2 to 3 of 4 at 5 in 6 about 7 with 8 at, at

131.4 2 John seems to be very keen on motor racing. 3 The three dogs are very important to my mother. 4 The circus isn't very popular with children nowadays. 5 Lucy has always been frightened of spiders. 6 Duncan was sorry about his mistake. 7 Clare is worried about tomorrow's exam. 8 Everyone was critical of the government's housing policy.

132.1 2 were you up to 3 's off 4 's been over 5 was, up to 6 is on

132.2 2 back 3 round 4 up 5 down 6 out 7 up 8 up

132.3 2 catch 3 carry 4 call 5 carry

132.4 2 up 3 in 4 out 5 on 6 up

132.5 2 up 3 in 4 up 5 off 6 up, down

132.6 2 do 3 fill 4 drop 5 do 6 drop

132.7 2 away 3 back 4 by 5 on 6 up 7 away with

132.8 2 give up 3 give out 4 gave in

132.9 2 off 3 out 4 down 5 off

132.10 2 a 3 b 4 c 5 d

132.11 2 up 3 out 4 up 5 up

132.12 2 up 3 out 4 out of 5 down 6 in 7 up with

132.13 2 look, up 3 make out 4 pick up 5 put off 6 taking off 7 turn down 8 make up

132.14 2 down 3 off 4 off 5 up 6 to

R25.1 2 either 3 Although 4 neither 5 Both 6 Despite

R25.2 2 so 3 therefore 4 so as not 5 in order to 6 so that

R25.3 2 until 3 After 4 as long as 5 before 6 as soon as

R25.4 2 trivial 3 annoying 4 noise 5 stand 6 Finally 7 bear 8 floor

R25.5 2 unless 3 Besides 4 like 5 than 6 provided

R25.6 2 imperfect 3 unbelievable 4 irrational 5 illiterate 6 incorrect

R25.7 2 education 3 enjoyment 4 hardship 5 performance 6 sisterhood 7 establishment 8 liberation 9 possibility 10 kindness 11 endurance 12 friendship 13 credibility 14 leadership

R25.8 2 She looked up the train times on the Internet. 3 Could you put me up for two nights next week? 4 Alison took up golf when she retired last year. 5 I usually turn on the radio when I'm in the kitchen. 6 We ran out of petrol twice last week. 7 It's a good idea to give up smoking. 8 I can't do without coffee in the morning.

N.1 2 C 3 D 4 A 5 C 6 D 7 A 8 A 9 A 10 B

N.2 2 she went out/going out 3 being 4 run as fast 5 as not to 6 we wanted to

N.3 Student's own answer.

N.4 2 on 3 Besides 4 also 5 away 6 Because 7 up 8 as 9 without 10 after 11 Despite 12 which

N.5 2 misunderstandings 3 unbelievable 4 independence 5 protective 6 different

N.6 2 In spite of 3 as a result 4 so wonderful that 5 Before settling down 6 In addition to not reading

p.359 1 thing 2 thin 3 seen 4 since 5 find 6 fine 7 pot 8 port 9 fire 10 fear 11 boot 12 but

p.359 1 We are in the garden. 2 Do you understand? 3 I love chocolate. 4 You can use my dictionary. 5 Where is the jam jar? 6 They watched television for two hours. 7 She wouldn't like to come to the beach. 8 You've got a nice bracelet. 9 He ran to catch the bus. 10 It was cold, dark and raining. 11 I'm sure they are English. 12 Thanks, these things belong to me.

p.359 3 1 /n/ 2 /f/ 3 /aɪ/ 4 /s/ 5 /θ/ 6 /ð/

p.359 4 1 /m/ 2 /tʃ/ 3 /θ/ 4 /dʒ/ 5 /ʃ/ 6 /θ/

TOP Grammar is a grammar reference book for students of English from **elementary level (A1)** to **upper-intermediate level (B2)**. It is comprehensive, clear, flexible and easy to use.

TOP Grammar is ideal for individual study, for use in class or for exam preparation.

TOP Grammar offers the student clear **grammar explanations with examples and more than 900 exercises**. Each of the 132 units is clearly laid out, with grammar rules on the left and exercises on the right. Each unit, as well as a grammar focus, covers a specific lexical area.

At the end of each of the 25 sections, there is a two-page Review with revision exercises.

There are also 14 sections of exam exercises that **prepare the student for PET and FCE exams**.

TOP Grammar components:
- **Student's Book**
- **CD-ROM** with 300 extra exercises and pronunciation, vocabulary and dictation practice
- **Teacher's Book** with
  - teaching tips for using TOP Grammar at home and in the class
  - 25 tests, one for each grammar section
  - Answer key to all the exercises and tests

Answer key also available as a separate booklet.

TOP Grammar

ISBN 978-3-85272-225-2

9 783852 722252

TOP Grammar
Student's Book
+ CD-ROM +
Answer Keys

HELBLING
LANGUAGES